# GAY MEN
## AND
# SUBSTANCE
# ABUSE

A Basic Guide for Addicts
and Those Who Care for Them

## MICHAEL SHELTON
### M.S., C.A.C.

Hazelden
Publishing

Hazelden Publishing
Center City, Minnesota 55012
hazelden.org/bookstore

© 2011 by Michael Shelton
All rights reserved. Published 2011
Printed in the United States of America

Library of Congress Cataloging-in-Publication Data

Shelton, Michael, 1965–
   Gay men and substance abuse : a basic guide for addicts and those who care
   for them / Michael Shelton.
      p.  cm.
   Includes bibliographical references.
   ISBN 978-1-59285-889-7
   1. Gay men—Substance use. 2. Gay men—Alcohol use. 3. Gay men—Drug use.
   4. Alcoholics—Rehabilitation. 5. Drug addicts—Rehabilitation. I. Title.
   HV5139.S54 2011
   616.86'06086642—dc22

                                            2010045849

**Editor's note**

The names, details, and circumstances may have been changed to protect the privacy of those mentioned in this publication.

This publication is not intended as a substitute for the advice of health care professionals.

21   2

Cover design by David Spohn
Interior design and typesetting by Percolator Graphic Design

*For Donald: the co-creator of all that is best in my life*

# CONTENTS

# ACKNOWLEDGMENTS

THANKS TO SID FARRAR and Patricia Boland at Hazelden for allowing this project to come to fruition, and to the following who offered their support and permission to use their materials: Sandra Anderson, Dana Finnegan, Jeff and Debra Jay, Sheppard Kominars, Duncan Osborne, Joseph Nowinski, Joe Amico, Penny Ziegler, and the staffs of tweaker.org and the Sexuality Information and Education Council of the United States (SIECUS).

# INTRODUCTION

THIS BOOK IS FOR GAY MEN who are struggling with substance abuse problems, as well as their loved ones, their partners and family members, and the helping professionals who work with them as therapists, social workers, medical doctors, clergy, or other counselors. The information in this book is intended to help the above audience make informed choices as they struggle to understand and make good decisions about dealing with a substance abuse problem. Since few people who are abusing substances seek out literature on the subject, they will probably read this book only when their loved ones and caregivers encourage them to learn more about their condition as a part of their decision-making process to seek help. While addiction professionals will be familiar with most of the basic information on substance abuse, they should find the sections specific to working with gay men enlightening.

Gay men, their partners, and family members often receive substandard and disrespectful treatment for substance abuse. I wrote this book to offer accurate and current information specific to their needs. All too frequently, knowledge about gay men is minimal in treatment facilities; counseling groups assume that members are heterosexual; staff and other clients look askance at sexual minorities; and their families are forgotten in planning interventions. Unless a gay male and his loved ones can afford the services of a treatment center targeting gay men (often $1,000 per day for residential services), he will likely end up in a public facility with varying degrees of experience, skill, and even interest in working with him and his loved ones. Gay men and the important people in their lives deserve better, and this book will guide you in making sure this happens, whether you are a loved one, a helping professional, or a gay male substance abuser seeking help.

## The Importance of Involving
## Loved Ones in Treatment

A gay man with substance abuse problems is all too often squeezed between two forces: a treatment system that doesn't know what to do with
him and a family system that cannot accept his sexuality, let alone his
drug abuse problem. Research increasingly shows the value of involving the family during treatment, but this invaluable opportunity may be
closed to gay men when treatment doesn't even recognize the existence
of their nontraditional families.

Counselors, or helping professionals of any kind, need to not only understand the complexity and intricacies of gay male drug use and its close
ties with sexual behavior, but also realize how the constellation of people
in a gay man's life can support his recovery. If a clinician doesn't know
how to work with a gay man individually, he or she will be even more at a
loss when the family enters the office. Working with gay men and addiction problems entails being able to talk knowledgeably, and with care and
sensitivity, about sexual orientation, heterosexism, homophobia, and sex
practices—all topics the clinician, the family, and the gay man himself
may be uncomfortable discussing.

Concerned others who will find the book helpful may be lovers, close
friends, and any family members who are interested in, and willing to
learn about, their loved one's lifestyle, drug use, and the history of their
problem.

Often, there are also family members who care deeply about their
loved one but from a removed position. They may be uncomfortable with
his sexual orientation, but love him and want him to be happy. Although
these family members may be uncomfortable with some of the sexually
explicit language in this book, they will nonetheless find information
here that can help them understand their loved one's motivation and the
challenges of recovery.

## Helping Professionals

Anyone entering treatment for a drug or alcohol problem is asked to
describe his or her life history. Typically only two questions about sex are
included in the inquiry:

• Are you a victim of sexual abuse?

• What is your sexual orientation?

Addictions professionals often understand their role in trauma work, and victims of past and current sexual abuse are offered at least cursory treatment materials even if the professional does not specialize in trauma work. Yet the second question—what is your sexual orientation—leaves most professionals stumped when the response is anything but straight. What are they supposed to do with this information? Does the person's sexuality in any way impact the substance use? And if it does, what can they offer to help? Sadly, this basic question is often simply ignored in the history-taking process. Even experienced clinicians may skip over the question and simply check "straight" or "heterosexual." Their own discomfort with the topic leads them to overlook sexuality. And of course gay men themselves often answer the question dishonestly. This may be due to their own shame issues or the seeming disapproval of the clinician (or both).

The fact that gay men often fail to identify themselves as such when they enter treatment, combined with the lack of research on gay populations in general and gay substance abusers in particular (resulting in a lack of knowledge by professionals), *and* the implied heterosexism in treatment facilities, a gay man seeking help for a drug use problem may have a bitter and unpleasant treatment experience. Many will never address their sexual orientation in treatment, whether this is in an inpatient or outpatient setting.

:::

Helping professionals, family, friends, and romantic partners will all find this book informative. A gay male seeking help for a substance abuse problem may be the last person to advocate for his own care and might not even recognize substandard treatment when he experiences it. While it is ultimately his decision to stop using substances, professionals and loved ones can work toward removing as many obstacles as possible to aid in his recovery efforts.

## CHAPTER ONE

# A Primer on Gay Men and Substance Abuse

THIS CHAPTER EXPLORES how gay men and men who have sex with other men develop substance abuse problems. It is not due, of course, to a moral failing, laziness, or even a lack of willpower. I have never worked with a man who planned on becoming an addict; all begin with a belief that they can control their use and that it will never become a problem.

## IN THE BEGINNING

Why does a gay man begin to use drugs and alcohol? Many of the reasons are the same as for anyone who uses substances, but some are more specific to gay men. The reasons below include both.

**To feel good.** Most abused drugs produce intense feelings of pleasure. Depending on the drug, users can feel euphoric and more powerful, self-confident, relaxed, and energetic than they usually feel.

**To feel better.** Drug use is "a means of changing one's experience of the world, whatever that experience may be for a particular individual . . . some individuals use drugs or engage in addictive behaviors not because *it makes them feel good*, but because it makes them *feel less bad* or, perhaps, *not feel at all*."[1] Drug use can reduce stress, anxiety, chronic pain, embarrassment, and shame. More than half of people with substance abuse problems have a chronic mental health issue, including depression, bipolar disorder, and anxiety.[2] Social difficulties commonly predate substance abuse. For the man terrified of approaching a stranger in a bar, a few drinks will bolster his courage.

**To do better and look better.** Gay athletes, like other athletes, use drugs such as steroids to enhance their performance, but also for aesthetic reasons—to pack on muscle mass and look more desirable to a potential dating or sex partner. Male body image is an important factor in the gay male bar scene—if you don't look hot, you'll have a tougher time finding a partner.

**To enhance sexual pleasure.** For many gay men, sexual activity goes hand in hand with drug and alcohol use. Many drugs heighten sexual arousal and extend performance. As a result, sober sexual activity may seem boring and bland.

**Curiosity and "because others are doing it."** One of the strongest predictors of substance use for adolescents is use by friends and acquaintances. If friends both approve of and use drugs, it is difficult for an adolescent to avoid doing so as well. A similar pattern exists for gay men. Much of gay male socializing occurs in settings in which substance use, particularly alcohol, is prevalent. Indeed, gay bars are often the social setting in which many gay men feel "most at home." Other settings include bathhouses, private house parties, and gigantic circuit parties (a large dance party that extends through the entire night and is preceded and followed by smaller events) that are held across the country (and even the world). All of these settings are replete with substance abuse.

**Shame.** Substance use is common during the coming-out process since, for so many gay men, this is a stressful time. Being a sexual minority is confusing and frightening, and drug use is one means of succor. Sadly, for gay men who struggle with their homosexuality, drug use often helps them hide from themselves, deny their same-sex yearnings, and cover up those conflicts. Many gay men began using substances at a very young age as they grappled with the confusion of being "different" from their peers. Some gay men hate themselves and are repulsed by their own sexual identity. This topic is discussed in chapter 3.

**Delayed adolescence.** The majority of straight men and women date and begin experimenting sexually during adolescence. The same is rarely true when it comes to gay men: gay adolescents have far fewer opportunities for dating simply because they are a minority and not surrounded by obvious and viable dating partners. In addition, the discomfort many gay male adolescents feel about their sexuality prevents them from opening up to other male adolescents who might have an interest. Because so few gay men experiment with dating in their teenage years, many experience a sort of delayed adolescence in their twenties and thirties when they begin to explore romantic relationships and sexual activity. Once they finally do begin to experiment, gay men are often flushed with excitement at their freedom to express the sexual urges and longings they so carefully hid in their younger years. As they abandon their repression, they embrace their new identity and participate in a wide array of gay male activities. This release from boundaries often includes substance use.

Of course, not every person goes on to develop a substance abuse problem. Even gay men from strikingly similar backgrounds who begin using drugs at the same age have vastly different long-term experiences with substance use. Most will use only recreationally for the rest of their lives, some will stop completely, and a few will experience significant problems related to their use. Even the most shame-cloaked man who lives his day-to-day life hiding in the shadows and uses drugs and alcohol to manage the terror of his sexual identity will not necessarily become an addict. If almost all gay men begin using substances for one (or more) of the reasons listed above, why do only a few experience severe consequences? What is different about those men?

## A DISEASE OF THE BRAIN

On a typical Friday night at one gay bar in Philadelphia, at least several hundred men pass through the doors before they close at 2 a.m. In the five-hour period before last call, the crowd will be buying drinks as fast as the bartenders can make them. On my last visit there it seemed as if every other person had a drink in their hands (and a cigarette in the other). Yet, the majority of these men do *not* have a substance abuse problem. Even those slobbering men who can barely remain upright on their stools are probably not alcoholics. Ditto for men across the country on that same evening who are smoking marijuana, downing Ecstasy or Xanax, snorting cocaine, or injecting meth. Ironically, some of the men in the bar who aren't drinking actually are alcoholics. Using one or more addictive substances does not make you an addict.

At this point you might conclude that it's the quantity of substances used that indicates addiction: If a person is using of lot of alcohol or other drugs, then they are probably addicted. This may be true in some cases, but other times it's completely wrong. Many, many gay men go through a period in their lives when their substance use escalates. I see this frequently in men who are in the process of coming out and who embrace the bar and club scene as their major recreational outlet. They may go quickly from drinking once or twice a year to spending every Friday and Saturday night in a drug-induced fog. Still, the quantity of substances used is not an automatic link with addiction. Addiction also does not necessarily follow a linear progression in which recreational use devolves into abuse and finally addiction. Most gay men who use drugs (even a lot of drugs) *do not* go on to abuse them; the majority will never experience any serious consequences from this use.

If a large quantity of substance use isn't a definitive marker for addiction, is a man an addict if he uses one or more addictive substances *and* has serious consequences from his use? Maybe. The combination of drug use and consequences is a starting point for a clinical diagnosis. But even this definition is not an unyielding rule. What looks like addiction could be a combination of drug use and impulsivity, bad judgment, bad luck, or just plain old stupidity. Consider Patrick. He interviewed at an investment firm and was relieved that the process went quite well. The interviewer told Patrick it would take at least a month before he made a hiring decision because there were so many candidates for the position.

After the interview, as he had planned, Patrick traveled to a beach house that belonged to his friend's parents, and the small gaggle of assembled friends quickly morphed into a rather gargantuan event. Patrick did imbibe that night—he smoked marijuana and ingested a "Xannie [Xanax] or two." He was certainly not unfamiliar with these drugs, but his use occurred at most six times a year and never led to complications. Imagine his alarm when the interviewer called the following Monday offering him the job with two caveats: background clearances and a urine test. He needed to give a sample within the next few days. Although Patrick drank as much water as he could over the next two days to flush out his system, the urine test still detected the presence of marijuana. Patrick did not get the job.

Did this make him an addict? A diagnosis requires a combination of substance use and consequences, and Patrick did indeed lose a job he both needed and wanted. In reality, however, his predicament was a combination of recreational use, bad judgment, and bad timing; it does not necessarily indicate addiction or even drug use problems (as defined by accepted clinical criteria). Consider that people overdose and even die every week from their first experimentation with drugs and alcohol.

Returning from a graduation party, the eighteen-year-old son of a friend was driving drunk when he lost control of the wheel, killing himself and two other young men. Friends later reported that this was the first time the young man had ever drank alcohol, and he had been giddy with inebriation before he left the party. Most of us would agree that death and manslaughter rank as extremely serious consequences of substance use, but in this young man's case the tragic consequences still do not qualify as addiction. It was a combination of substance use, youthful exuberance, lack of experience with alcohol, and overconfidence in his ability to drive after drinking.

What, then, is addiction? Those who adhere to the Twelve Step principles often state that they have an "allergy" to drugs of abuse. This is not technically true, but it does help illustrate the concept of addiction. When addicts come into contact with one or more substances—by ingesting, snorting, smoking, injecting, inhaling, or any other method of use—their brains react in a vastly different way than do the brains of non-addicts. While both the addict and the non-addict may speed up, slow down, hallucinate, or zone out dependent on what drug they are using, for the addict something else happens in the brain. This "something else" does not happen to recreational drug users or even abusers. And it is this difference in addicts' brains that is key to today's definition of addiction: addiction is a combination of substance use, consequences, and an individual's brain functioning.

The definition began to take shape approximately twenty years ago when the U.S. National Institute on Drug Abuse (NIDA) began promoting a new theory of addiction, one that is very different from earlier models that viewed it as a moral failing or one requiring spiritual triage (as with the Twelve Step model). NIDA defines addiction as "a chronic, relapsing brain disease that is characterized by compulsive drug seeking and use, despite harmful consequences."[3]

Let's look at how brain functioning comes into play with addiction. All drugs of abuse directly or indirectly target the reward system of the brain by flooding the circuit with the neurotransmitter dopamine.

Dopamine is a natural chemical in the brain that makes us feel good. For most people, dopamine levels rise when they eat good food, have sex, or engage in other activities they find pleasurable. When our system is flooded with dopamine and we feel great, we're motivated to do, and/or continue doing, whatever is producing that dopamine. Unfortunately, the feel-good chemicals produced by *naturally* rewarding behaviors don't begin to compare with how drug use affects the brain's pleasure circuit. Indeed, drug use triggers the release of an excess amount of dopamine, overstimulating the reward system and producing a euphoric effect. Such a powerful reward is what teaches people who abuse drugs to repeat the behavior. They are strongly motivated to take drugs again and again.

## WHAT IS SUBSTANCE ABUSE?

Recreational use, substance abuse, and addiction are vastly different categories, though some people use the latter two interchangeably. This may be fine in general, but if you have a substance use problem it really does help to know which category best identifies your pattern of use. Not only are typical outcomes different, but the changes you must make in your life are strikingly different.

To receive an official diagnosis of substance abuse, substance use must be recurring and causing problems in one's life—financial, legal, personal, and at work, school, or home.

It is also important to recognize the difference between "use" and "abuse." Substance *use* is such a prevalent aspect of life for so many gay men. And while many of these drugs are illegal, their use does not necessarily constitute diagnosable substance abuse. Cocaine is illegal, and the man who parties on this drug is committing a criminal act by simply possessing it (and even more if he distributes it to friends and sex partners), but unless it is causing challenges and complications in his life, he would not be diagnosed with a substance abuse disorder. He is a recreational drug user. However, if this same man finds that under the influence of cocaine he has unintended unsafe sex and spends far more money than planned on several occasions, a clinical diagnosis might be warranted. Substance abuse is *a pattern* of damaging use. As a general rule, if drug or alcohol use is causing complications in life, even if they are only minor problems, this is a red flag that recreational use could be escalating into abuse.

As researchers continue to study the using patterns of gay men, we can expect to see addendums to the official diagnostic criteria for substance abuse. I propose, then, that the following four behaviors point toward substance abuse issues for gay men:

1. Recurrent unsafe sex while under the influence of one or more substances

2. Recurrent inability to perform sexually unless substance use occurs

3. Drug use that leads to medicine noncompliance

4. Drug use that leads to a change in lifestyle

### Recurrent Unsafe Sex While Under the Influence

Note the word "recurrent." When comparing gay men to other demographic groups (such as heterosexuals or lesbians), two patterns emerge. First, gay men tend to engage in far more anonymous sex. Second, their rate of infidelity while involved in romantic relationships is much higher. Today's general culture is sex saturated, and the gay male culture magnifies this even more.

The availability of numerous sex partners creates opportunities for sexual activity with men our loved one knows nothing about and may never see again. Yes, this offers ceaseless carnal novelty and pleasure, but it also jeopardizes his health. For too many gay men, contracting their first sexually transmitted disease is a rite of passage. All drugs can influence sexual decision making and behaviors, but let's look briefly at the one that receives the most attention in the media—methamphetamine.

Mansergh and colleagues found that use of meth doubled the likelihood that men would engage in unprotected anal intercourse,[4] and researcher Perry Halkitis reported that a shocking eighteen times more unprotected sex occurred between gay men using this drug.[5] In 2003 the *San Francisco Chronicle* reported that male recent meth users accounted for one-third of new HIV diagnoses.[6]

There are indeed men who do not care for safe sex, and substance use does not affect their decision making because they have no intention of practicing it (though substance use still increases their risk of disease, as it may lead to rougher sex and even more risky sexual activities). But if remaining disease free and minimizing risk *is* important for a gay man, and his substance use leads to unsafe practices, his drug use would be considered abusive, not recreational.

## Recurrent Inability to Perform Sexually unless Substance Use Occurs

For some gay men, being sexual with another man causes conflicted emotions. The activity is fraught with unpleasant emotions yet fueled and driven by an otherwise unquenchable arousal and desire. Many of my peers would conclude that shame plays no small role in the lives of these men. This is especially true for men who believe that same-sex activity is somehow wrong, "a sin," or unnatural. Many of these men would prefer to change their sexual orientation (and many have tried to do so without success). But such conflicted emotions over gay sexual activity are not always related to shame, and, of course, none of these is mutually exclusive.

For example, men who were sexually abused as children and/or experienced other sexual trauma often have difficulty experiencing pleasure in sex. This is true for men whether they're gay or straight. While some children who have been sexually abused become hypersexual as adults, many others limit their sexual activity, often to the point of celibacy.

Conflicted emotions regarding sex are also common for men who were raised with a negative view of sex in general, even if same-sex sexual activity was never discussed by caregivers. These men cannot help but feel conflicted in their same-sex sexual relationships; for them, all sexual activity is wrong. And yet another group—men who are timid, shy, and reserved by nature—may use drugs to "loosen" themselves up for sexual activity. Finally, men who doubt their ability to perform sexually may use drugs and alcohol to improve their skills. This last category has only recently received the attention of clinicians and researchers. A few studies have revealed that some men with substance abuse problems began using substances in order to enhance sexual performance.

All of these men use drugs to overcome profound issues such as shyness, inhibition, shame, doubt, and conflicted emotions. Drug use is, then, a form of self-medication to quell these emotions and fears and partake of sexual activity. Although occasionally using drugs and alcohol to heighten sexual experience is not unusual, when a man needs them for the majority of his sexual experiences, substance abuse is probable. Such an inability to have sex with another man unless under the influence of substances indicates not only substance abuse but also other significant problems.

## Drug Use That Leads to Medicine Noncompliance

While this section focuses on medications for HIV, it applies to all pre-scription medications. For those of us who lived through the bleak early days of the AIDS epidemic, the availability of any medication that could expand one's quality of life—even if only for several months—was cause for jubilation. Now with over thirty medications available targeting dif-ferent events in the virus's lifecycle, it seems, especially to many younger gay men, that the disease is without doubt manageable if not outright conquered. Not surprisingly, then, recent surveys and polls of gay men tell us that less-safe sexual practices are again on the rise in tandem with an increase in the HIV rate. Men who do have HIV try to not skip doses—despite the often unpleasant side effects of many of these meds— because of HIV's ability to develop resistance to these drugs. Unfortu-nately, missed doses of medication can hasten the time frame for resis-tance from years to months. Some practitioners warn that with even one or two missed doses, the virus may begin to develop resistance.

Let's go back to methamphetamine again. One study by Halkitis and colleagues found that gay and bisexual men who use meth miss more doses of their medication than those who did not use drugs (twelve missed doses versus four in a two-month period).[7]

I work with substance-abusing gay men who are resistant to every drug that is available to treat HIV and who now peg their hopes on new pharmaceuticals descending down the research pipeline. Many in the field question the wisdom of offering HIV drugs to an active substance abuser who cannot or will not follow through on the medication regimen. Not only is this idea of withholding medications a threat to the substance abuser's health, it also poses a risk to the gay community as a whole. Gay men who grow resistant to one or more drugs (and even entire classes of drugs) and practice unsafe sex can pass on these resistant viruses to other men. If substance use is interfering with medication compliance for any prescription medication regimen, I recommend that the man have an honest discussion with a health care provider who can point out the many, many negative consequences of using substances along with prescribed medications. And if noncompliance has already played a role in resistance to several medications, it's time to ask him this question: Has your substance use morphed into substance abuse?

Finally, if substance use in any way negatively impacts a pre-existing health problem, the red flag of possible abuse is up. For example, all stimulant drugs lead to higher systemic HIV viral loads, and meth in particular is associated with more HIV viral replication in the brain, even if that person is taking their medications religiously.

## Drug Use That Leads to a Change in Lifestyle

Researchers use the jargon "narrowing of behavioral and environmental repertoires" to describe the process by which activities and pastimes that don't involve drug use fade away and are replaced by those related to substance use. In his book *Addiction and Change,* renowned substance abuse researcher Carlo C. DiClemente offers this analogy:

> Since the arrival of our second child, my wife and I are preoccupied with taking care of and being with the children during our free time; non-child oriented activities have moved more and more into the background. The narrowing of the behaviors is simply a natural part of becoming preoccupied with a preferred activity. Similarly, as an individual becomes more and more involved with an addictive behavior, it becomes a priority to seek opportunities to engage in the behavior and associate with others who share the behavior.[8]

If his recreational pastimes, interests, and range of friends have become increasingly narrow and centered on alcohol or other drug use, then this, too, indicates that his use is progressing into abuse. Even if substance use has not led to any problems in his life, the narrowing of his lifestyle in order *to incorporate substance use* is a warning sign that future problems await.

Substance abuse, then, is a pattern of drug use leading to recurrent and significant problems in one's life. An important point to keep in mind—and one that differentiates abuse from addiction—is that substance use is voluntary. He can put alcohol and other drugs down. He can stop on his own. He might like the effects of his chosen substance(s), but he has the willpower to end his use when the consequences are severe enough. This aspect of choice is what is missing in addiction, our next topic.

# WHAT IS ADDICTION?

People entering treatment for substance use receive a diagnosis of either "abuse" or "dependence." However, for this chapter we will use the word "addiction" instead of "dependence," as it is much more recognized and understood.

While substance abuse is diagnosed by evidence of significant adverse consequences of repeated drug use, addiction is characterized by compulsive use. If a man recognizes the serious consequences of his drug use and, as a result, stops completely or even successfully cuts backs on his use, a diagnosis of abuse is appropriate. On the other hand, if a man recognizes the serious consequences of his drug use but cannot stop despite concerted efforts and a sincere desire to do so, we are now discussing addiction. Addiction, then, is evident when even the most serious and looming consequences are not enough to halt a person's substance use.

Tolerance and withdrawal are often considered hallmarks of addiction; however, neither of these has to be present, nor does their presence unfailingly signal addiction. The definition of tolerance is when you need more of a substance, or different combinations of drugs, in order to get the same high. When my partner had surgery necessitating a deep incision along the length of his abdomen, he was given morphine for the intense pain. Over a period of a week, he became tolerant of the medication and needed higher doses for the same ameliorative effect. He also experienced unpleasant withdrawal symptoms for several days when he stopped taking the morphine. Yet he was by no means an addict.

Indeed, it's possible to be physically dependent and quickly develop tolerance for many substances without experiencing significant impairment or distress as a result. For example, a person may take medications as prescribed and, when they are no longer needed, cope with the discomfort of withdrawal and then go on with his life. But if these same drugs become the focus of the person's life, negatively affecting his lifestyle and leading to questionable activities to obtain them (such as forged doctors' prescriptions), active addiction is at play.

Addiction is probable if a man has made several unsuccessful attempts at ending or controlling his drug use and continues to use in spite of escalating repercussions. When substance use dominates a person's life, addiction is evident. The Twelve Step literature offers markers for addiction, signals that are hinted at in the clinical literature but need further elaboration. The first is the concept of "powerlessness." In short, addicts have lost the power to control and moderate their substance use.

Many people struggling with addiction issues fail to recognize the role of powerlessness in their own lives because they misunderstand the concept. It does not mean they have lost complete power over all aspects of their lives (though escalating use often does lead to serious complications). Often, for example, addicts can continue to function in the workplace or maintain family responsibilities, at least for a while, even if their performance has deteriorated. Nor does powerlessness mean that one is utterly helpless when confronted with alcohol and drugs. Being offered an alcoholic drink at a wedding or a snort of cocaine on the dance floor does not necessarily lead to its use. Indeed, many addicts can turn away without challenge (though many might succumb to the temptation).

Powerlessness instead means that when the addict picks up a drink, that line of coke, or any other substance available, he cannot consistently stop himself from further use and the resulting problems. That one drink is now a weekend binge. That line of coke leads to meth use and unplanned, unsafe sexual activity. An addict promises himself "this time it will be different—I will control myself." But once he starts, these promises (to himself and others) are now a crapshoot.

Powerlessness is the acceptance that once you ingest a chosen substance, the outcomes are unpredictable. The Big Book of Alcoholics Anonymous (AA) offers an accurate description of repeated failed attempts at controlling and ending alcohol use that can be generalized to all men and women with substance abuse issues:

> Here are some of the methods we have tried: Drinking beer only, limiting the number of drinks, never drinking alone, never drinking in the morning, drinking only at home, never having it in the house, never drinking during business hours, drinking only at parties, switching from scotch to brandy, drinking only natural wines, agreeing to resign if ever drunk on the job, swearing off forever (with or without a solemn oath), taking more physical exercise, reading inspirational books . . . we could increase the list ad infinitum.[9]

If a man has tried to control or stop his substance use and failed; made oaths and failed; modified his environment, friends, and social life and still failed; experimented with several different "cures" from the medical to the new age and failed, it is then likely he has an addiction.

Another marker for addiction is the unmanageability of daily life due to the compounding of negative consequences stemming from his substance use. By the time a man has developed compulsive drug use, the quality of his life has typically eroded. His relationships are floundering, his work is increasingly difficult and marked by poor performance, and he is experiencing legal and financial problems. At the same time, he has less energy, motivation, and/or desire to even begin dealing with these problems. In short, problems and complications from substance use have overwhelmed his life. He looks back in retrospect and wonders just how he could sink this far in such a seemingly short period of time.

:: 

A maxim of Twelve Step groups is that addicts are not responsible for having an addiction, but they are responsible for dealing with it. Many might argue this point and claim that gay men really are to blame for an addiction because they started using drugs and alcohol in the first place—if they had never started experimenting with these substances, they would never have become addicted. While this argument makes sense at a superficial level, recreational substance use is so widespread and common for gay men that condemning someone for following the norm seems unjust. It is only after he has started using one or more substances that he recognizes that a problem exists.

After considering the information presented in this chapter, the question now is—how would you classify the substance use of the man you are concerned about? Is he a recreational user? Abuser? Addicted/dependent? Be aware that even recreational use can have its complications. If an employer requires a drug-free workplace, an employee's occasional marijuana use can lead to negative consequences if random urine tests are conducted. One night of binge drinking can lead to an automobile accident. A singular experiment with meth can lead to unsafe sex. Emergency room personnel are very familiar with overdoses stemming from a novice's attempt at drug use. A diagnosis has importance other than for naming purposes. It plays a decisive factor in setting goals, most obviously controlled use or lifelong abstinence. These are considerations we take up in the following chapters.

## CHAPTER TWO

# PARTY AND PLAY

SANDRA ANDERSON, author of *Substance Use Disorders in Lesbian, Gay, Bisexual, and Transgender Clients*, believes that one of the most pressing challenges for gay male substance abusers is to decouple, or separate, sexual activity from substance use.[1] For many gay men, the two go hand in hand and are such a long-standing part of their lives that a division between the two seems almost impossible. A common question I hear is, "How will I enjoy sex without drugs and alcohol?" Separating the two activities is often a major issue in treatment and recovery. As the last chapter discussed, for some gay men, their internalized heterosexism makes sexual contact with another man almost impossible without some form of substance to facilitate the experience. Others have learned that the use of one or more substances (particularly those highlighted in this chapter) makes sex more intense and exciting; sex without substance use simply cannot compare. Often these two seemingly disparate categories of gay men actually converge in one person: a gay man who is deeply ashamed of his identity but who is nonetheless hooked on the exhilaration of drug-enhanced sexual activity.

For helping professionals and others concerned about gay male substance abusers and addicts, there is this challenge: to accept the gay man's decisions regarding his sexual life. Even when he quits using substances, he may continue to engage in sexual practices considered high risk and, for many, "distasteful," "sinful," and even "disgusting," adjectives I have heard many times from concerned family members. Some family members want their loved one to not only stop using drugs but also to stop being gay. And though the latter isn't possible (and more and more family members are recognizing that such a conversion isn't going to happen), they at least want him to stop engaging in sexual activity with other men. In essence, the implicit or explicit message is that being gay is beyond your control, but "acting" gay is certainly a choice, and acting gay is most evident in sexual behaviors.

This chapter presents an overview of drugs most associated with sexual activity for gay men. Indeed, the title of this chapter, "Party and Play," is a common phrase in the gay community, referring to drug use and sexual activity. Some readers will shrug their shoulders and mutter "what's the big deal?" and possibly even recognize some aspects of their own lifestyle in the following pages. Others, though, may find the material a litmus test for their ability to consider sexual activity and gay men. It is these latter readers who may need to make far-reaching adjustments in order to understand the addictive patterns of gay men. Assisting them in recovery means addressing the topic of sexuality, and this includes sexual activity, a topic many readers will undoubtedly shy away from.

A warning before we continue: Since drug use is so linked to sexual activity in gay male social circles, the first-person reports I use contain some sexually explicit language.

## DRUGS AND SEX

It is impossible to discuss gay men and substance use without highlighting club drugs, methamphetamine, and poppers. Gay male substance abusers can certainly have problems with any class of drugs. I have worked with those addicted to heroin, prescription medications, marijuana, cocaine, and alcohol. Still, when gay men and substances are discussed in the mainstream media, inevitably you will hear about club drugs, methamphetamine, poppers, and unsafe sex. And there is no doubt that these drugs destroy the lives of many a gay man each and every year. Indeed, if you attend a Narcotics Anonymous (NA) meeting targeting gay men in any large city, the majority of participants will be there for meth. In regard to the club drugs, many gay men are unaware of both their acute dangers and long-term repercussions, particularly toxicity to the brain. And as to methamphetamine, it is shocking how quickly it can completely take over a gay man's life. Most people are aware of the addictive potential of crack cocaine, but meth addiction likewise develops rapidly.

It is impossible to have a comprehensive discussion of these drugs without exploring sexual behavior. Pointedly, the substances highlighted in this chapter are often taken in tandem with Viagra, that well-known and well-advertised erectile dysfunction drug. Abuse of this drug has escalated among all men, but particularly so among gay men. Men report that Viagra not only produces a thicker-looking penis (due to the engorged blood supply), but that it enables them to continue on with sexual activity long past the point where they would otherwise stop. In circuit parties, dance clubs, bathhouses, and private parties, participants use multiple club drugs (often more than one), methamphetamine, alcohol, poppers, and maybe even some cocaine all in the same evening. Several studies find that men who engage in such activity tend to have more sexual partners, more unprotected sex, and more sexually transmitted diseases.

It is important to understand just how difficult it might be for a gay man to sever the connection between drug use and sex. Let's look more closely at the biological underpinnings of this challenge. Drugs of abuse work in the brain by tapping into the brain's communication system and interfering with the way nerve cells send and receive information. As we discussed in chapter 1, all drugs of abuse directly or indirectly target the limbic system—the reward center of the brain—by flooding it with the neurotrasmitter dopamine.

The limbic system is the same area of the brain stimulated by sexual activity. However, when some drugs of abuse are taken, they can release *two to ten times* the amount of dopamine that natural rewards do. In an apt comparison offered by the National Institute on Drug Abuse (NIDA), the difference in effect is the difference between someone whispering into your ear and someone shouting into a microphone. The resulting effects on the brain's pleasure circuit dwarf those produced by naturally rewarding behaviors such as eating and sex. The effect of such a powerful reward strongly motivates people to take drugs again and again.

In treatment and support groups, addicts are taught to avoid relapse by listing all of the high-risk scenarios they once associated with substance use. However, the effect of the drug is so powerful on the brain that even seemingly irrelevant stimuli can lead to what seems inexplicable craving. To illustrate, let's first revisit some basic high school science: conditioning. In Pavlov's famous experiment, dogs not only began to salivate when they saw food, but after being fed by the same lab technician for several days, these same dogs began to salivate when they saw him, even if no food was present. The dogs had learned to associate this person with food. Cat owners recognize that the sound of an electric can opener is a clarion call to any felines in the domicile; cats (and dogs) learn to associate the whirring of the can opener with food.

Our growing understanding of the molecular complexity of conditioning leaves no doubt that drug-environment associations have a direct effect on specific brain regions and circuitry, and this has profound implications for those in recovery. Drug use leads to a wide variety of stimuli—different for each person—that creates strong cravings for the drug, even after an extended period of abstinence. These cravings are so strong that they can even lead to a return of withdrawal symptoms. Or, as explained by Dr. George Koob at Scripps Research Institute regarding his NIDA-funded research:

> Imagine a drug user who usually buys cocaine at a particular subway stop and typically experiences a drug effect shortly after the purchase. Eventually, the subway stop—normally a neutral part of the environment—becomes linked in the mind of the drug user to the positive rewarding effects of cocaine. Later, even after successful treatment for drug abuse, the sight of the subway stop can bring on craving for cocaine. That is, the subway stop has become a conditioned stimulus that may trigger relapse.[2]

Gay men who use drugs in combination with sex have formed, in their brains, an association between the two that will be difficult to recalibrate, especially in the early stages of recovery. This is why even a brief episode of sexual arousal, such as seeing an attractive person on the street, can lead to seemingly irresistible cravings for drug use and all too often a relapse. Conversely, many gay men complain that sexual activity without drug use is dull. As you will hear in this chapter, adding drug use to sexual activity leads to the best sex some men have ever had, and some will never be willing to give this up.

## Club Drugs

Circuit parties are extravagant dance events, often lasting through the night, that attract thousands to tens of thousands of participants. While open to anyone, the parties are generally social events for gay men, and these lavish events contribute some of their proceeds to LGBT nonprofit organizations. Attend one of these events and you will see thousands of sweaty, shirtless gay men writhing to the DJ- supplied music. Many of the men will have taken one or more of the most common club drugs.

Here are the most widely used club drugs:

**GHB** (gamma-hydroxybutyrate), or **Xyrem,** is a central nervous system depressant that was approved by the Food and Drug Administration (FDA) in 2002 for use in the treatment of narcolepsy (a sleep disorder). This approval came with severe restrictions, including its use only for the treatment of narcolepsy, and the requirement for a patient registry monitored by the FDA. GHB also has anabolic effects (helps build muscle) and so is used by gay men to both increase muscle size and to lose fat. At high doses, GHB's sedative effects may result in sleep, coma, or death.

Street names for GHB: GHB, "G" (most common), Gamma-OH, Liquid E, Fantasy, Georgia Home Boy, Grievous Bodily Harm, Liquid X, Liquid Ecstasy (it is *not* Ecstasy), Scoop, Water, Everclear, Great Hormones at Bedtime, GBH, Soap, Easy Lay, Salty Water, G-Riffick, Cherry Meth, Organic Quaalude, and Jib.

**Rohypnol** (flunitrazepam) started appearing in the United States in the early 1990s. It is a benzodiazepine (chemically similar to Valium or Xanax), but it is not approved for medical use in this country, and its importation is banned. Rohypnol is usually taken orally, although there are reports that it can be ground up and snorted. Rohypnol is most well known as the date rape drug, since it is colorless, tasteless, and odorless and can be added to drinks and ingested without the victim's knowledge. When mixed with alcohol, Rohypnol can incapacitate victims and prevent them from resisting sexual assault. Like other benzodiazepines, it can produce anterograde amnesia—this is when people may not remember events they experienced while under the influence of the drug.

Street names for Rohypnol: Rophy, Ruffles, Roofies, Ruffies, Ruff Up, Rib, Roach 2, R2, R2-Do-U, Roche, Rope, Ropies, Circles, Circes, Forget It, Forget-Me-pill, Mexican Valium.

**Ketamine** is a dissociative anesthetic, mostly used in veterinary practice, and is usually snorted or injected intramuscularly. It distorts perceptions of sight and sound and produces feelings of detachment from the environment and self. Low doses of ketamine result in impaired attention, learning ability, and memory. At higher doses, ketamine can cause dreamlike states and hallucinations; and at higher doses still, ketamine can cause delirium and amnesia.

Street names for ketamine: Special K, "K," Kit Kat, Cat Valium.

**MDMA** (methylenedioxymethamphetamine) has become a popular drug because of its positive effects experienced within an hour or so after taking a single dose. MDMA leads to euphoria, feelings of closeness and bonding, and a communal sharing of camaraderie and mutual understanding. It also leads to a general sense of well-being, decreased anxiety, disinhibition, and sexual activity—often of an unsafe nature. In addition, users report enhanced sensory perception as a hallmark of the MDMA experience. MDMA is also associated with vigorous physical activity for extended periods. It produces a variety of adverse health effects, including nausea, chills, sweating, involuntary teeth clenching, muscle cramping, and blurred vision. The symptoms of an MDMA overdose can include high blood pressure, faintness, panic attacks, and in severe cases, a loss of consciousness and seizures.

Street name for MDMA: Ecstasy.

Many men believe that club drugs are relatively safe in spite of the well-publicized deaths that occur with their use. Furthermore, many gay men believe that such drugs have low potential for addiction. The National Institute on Drug Abuse has done quite a bit of research over the past decade on club drug use, and the findings of these studies correct this misperception that club drugs are safe or that they have low potential for abuse and dependence. For example:

- One study found that 43 percent of those who reported MDMA use met the accepted diagnostic criteria for dependence—continued use despite knowledge of physical or psychological harm, withdrawal effects, and tolerance—and 34 percent met the criteria for drug abuse.[3]

- Almost 60 percent of people who use MDMA report withdrawal symptoms, including fatigue, loss of appetite, depressed feelings, and trouble concentrating.[4]

- Repeated use of GHB may lead to withdrawal effects, including insomnia, anxiety, tremors, and sweating. Severe withdrawal reactions have been reported among patients who have overdosed on

GHB or related compounds, especially when other drugs or alcohol were involved.

• As with other benzodiazepines, chronic use of Rohypnol can produce tolerance and dependence.

• There have been reports of people bingeing on ketamine, a behavior that is similar to that seen in some cocaine- or amphetamine-dependent people. Ketamine users can develop tolerance and cravings for the drug.

As with all drugs of potential abuse, simply using one or more of these substances does not indicate a diagnosable substance use problem. Remember, there must be compulsiveness, recurrent problems stemming from such use, tolerance, and/or withdrawal to meet the clinical standards of addiction. But if a man continues to risk his health via unsafe sex connected to drug use (and even men already infected with one or more sexually transmitted diseases risk further health damage with reinfection by a new partner), this indicates a serious substance use problem, not mere recreational use.

## Methamphetamine

Regular circuit party attendees (men who plan their yearly schedule around major party events and who attend as many as possible, or as many as they can afford, since these events are not inexpensive) have noted a shift in the scene. They report that although designer club drugs are certainly still available, methamphetamine has insidiously infiltrated these events and is changing the atmosphere of circuit parties—specifically, it is creating a far more aggressive sexual atmosphere.

Initially limited to Hawaii and western parts of the United States, methamphetamine has spread across the country. It is a highly addictive stimulant that can be snorted, smoked, injected, orally ingested, and even used rectally. Methamphetamine is commonly known as "speed," "meth," and "chalk," and in its smoked form, it is often referred to as "ice," "crystal," "crank," and "glass." In contrast to cocaine, which is quickly removed and almost completely metabolized in the body, methamphetamine's effects last much longer and a larger percentage of the drug remains unchanged in the body. This means that methamphetamine stays in the brain longer, which ultimately leads to prolonged stimulant effects.

Meth is commonly used along with club drugs and cocaine. Lately, many chronic meth users have added Viagra to the mix, since meth often leads to erectile difficulties. With chronic abuse, users can develop tolerance to methamphetamine's pleasurable effects. In an effort to intensify the desired effects, abusers may take higher doses of the drug, take it more frequently, or change their method of drug intake. When a chronic abuser stops taking the drug, he goes into withdrawal.

In his book *Suicide Tuesday: Gay Men and the Crystal Meth Scare*, Duncan Osborne begins with an apt description of meth withdrawal:

> The party begins on a Thursday or Friday with the first hit of crystal. It continues through the weekend with more meth and, many users will tell you, a great deal of the best sex they have ever had, often without condoms, and, just as often, with many men. Sleeping, eating, taking medications, either for HIV or for some other condition, may or may not be part of the weekend. By late Sunday or early Monday, the user will have had enough, but that does not mean that the effects of the drug will allow him to sleep. . . . A user will be physically exhausted, which is not surprising given the drug and sex marathon he has just run, but the effect is more than just extreme fatigue. . . . [The user experiences] an ugly crash that can include exhaustion and depression. It is called Suicide Tuesday because, as the name suggests, users feel so awful, they just want to die. For chronic meth users, the effect on the brain can grow making each succeeding Suicide Tuesday that much more intense and the desire to get high again that much greater.[5]

National Institute on Drug Abuse researchers originally thought that gay men abusing meth were self-medicating, that they were attempting to deal with underlying depression. After all, gay men are more likely than heterosexual men to be diagnosed with depression. These gay men often cited their ongoing struggle to live as a gay man in a heterosexist world as the source of their depression. However, studies did not find support for this theory but rather found some evidence that *most men continued to abuse meth to deal with the depressive symptoms brought on by withdrawal.*[6]

Meth users often stay awake for days (sometimes weeks) at a time, episodes that can lead to hospitalization for violent behavior, anxiety, delusions, and paranoia. Psychotic symptoms sometimes continue for months or years after methamphetamine abuse has stopped, and stress can trigger methamphetamine psychosis to recur in formerly psychotic methamphetamine abusers.

Meth can bring on cognitive and emotional deterioration. Recent studies find that chronic methamphetamine use leads to severe structural and functional changes in areas of the brain associated with emotion and memory, and indeed, chronic meth users do have many emotional and cognitive problems. Some of these brain regions did not recover even after two years of abstinence, indicating that some methamphetamine-induced changes are very long-lasting.[7]

Meth users report the following common side effects: weight loss, sleepiness, financial problems, paranoia, legal problems, hallucinations, work problems, violent behavior, and dental problems.

Meth is a particularly dangerous drug. With all of these consequences, why would gay men consider using methamphetamine? Even worse, why is meth use reaching nearly epidemic proportions in gay male communities across the United States? Tweaker.org, a web site promoting safe sex by gay meth users, listed the most common reasons for meth use:[8]

1. I do it for the high. The rush. The euphoria.

2. The SEX! For me, sex is synonymous with speed. And it's for the "freaky sex," going places I would never go without speed.

3. Endurance: To dance all night or all weekend—on the floor or between the sheets!

4. To be a bottom. It's the only way I can relax and enjoy receptive anal sex.

5. To ease social anxiety. Speed gives me an incredible sense of confidence and self-esteem. When I first did it, I thought "this is what I've been missing."

6. To fit in with the club scene guys and to pick up guys online who might not look at me otherwise.

7. The weight loss. Crystal meth curbs my appetite. It's the "Jenny Crank" Diet.

8. I do it to boost creativity with hobbies or art. Productivity at work. Or to do housecleaning or other repetitive tasks.

Overall, the most common reason men give for using meth is its impact on sex. Many report that meth leads to the best sex of their lives, including performance stamina, delayed ejaculation, and the ability to override any feelings of internalized heterosexism that could detract from their enjoyment. A 2007 study found that meth use not only increases sexual arousal and pleasure, but that it also temporarily clouded over any feelings of internalized heterosexism, sexual unattractiveness, and concerns about HIV.[9] Club drugs may heighten sexual experience, but they pale in comparison to meth. Let's examine another page from Tweaker.org in regard to sexual activity:[10]

Crystal meth has earned an infamous association with sex. After having sex on crystal, some guys find that plain old sex is boring, not intense enough, not exciting enough. Eventually some of us felt like we couldn't have sex without it. We might like being dominated in bed, but being dominated by crystal isn't fun for anyone.

Some of us use when we cruise because we find that meth heightens arousal and increases sexual stamina. There's also the delayed orgasm which makes play time go on and on and on. It's a big drag that impotence is a common side effect. This impotence is sometimes called crystal dick. You're sexually aroused but your cock won't cooperate; you can't keep it up or, even worse, get it up in the first place.

Crystal meth may increase your confidence at the same time it lowers inhibitions. Under the influence, we might give in to our impulses and do stuff we might not otherwise have done. There's a big risk of HIV infection through unprotected sex and perhaps more so while under the influence of meth. How come? Often enough, when we're zooming, everything we've been told, learned and practiced in terms of safe sex seems to be forgotten. And it's forgotten when we need it most because when we're high sexual activity and the desire for it increases like nobody's business. Some men who get fucked while they're high on speed are less sensitive to pain and may find themselves seeking out, asking for and having more aggressive sex for longer periods. Nothing wrong with an aggro-fuck now and again, but without feeling all of what's going on, injury is more likely to occur and the risk of HIV infection is increased.

I have worked with men who had long refused to have anal intercourse as the receptive partner, yet under the influence of meth not only
participate in just such activity but also without the use of a condom, and
repeatedly over the course of a weekend. Meth use doubles the likelihood
that a gay man will have unprotected receptive anal sex.

Methamphetamine cannot typically be used in moderation; it soon
begins to negatively affect all aspects of a gay man's life. Yes, there are
men who can party with meth occasionally without developing a substance abuse problem, but they are few. Because of the explosive impact
of meth on the brain, the potential for abuse and addiction is very high.
The sexual euphoria in combination with brain changes makes it impossible for many men to see this risk until the consequences are severe.

## Poppers

Poppers have never really caught on with straight men, but most gay
men, even if they haven't used them, are at least familiar with them. Poppers are classified by the National Institute on Drug Abuse (NIDA) as inhalants—volatile substances that produce chemical vapors that can be
inhaled to induce mind-altering effects. Other common inhalants include
paint thinners and removers, dry cleaning fluids, degreasers, gasoline,
correction fluids, felt-tip marker fluids, spray paint, and hair and deodor-
ant sprays.

Poppers are a special class of inhalants called nitrites, and they include amyl, butyl, and cyclohexyl nitrites. In the past, amyl nitrite, the
inhalant most common in the gay male community, was used to alleviate
chest pain and is sometimes used today for diagnostic purposes in heart
examinations.

In his book *Peek*, Joseph Couture wrote about his experience using poppers:[11] "One night I staggered home drunk from the bar, having
failed to pick up a trick, and fell into bed. I was jerking off with a bottle of poppers when I fell asleep before I finished with the bottle in my
hand. It leaked and I woke up in the middle of the night in horrible pain.
I had this large burn on my finger where the poppers had leaked out and
soaked into my hand. I went to the doctor the next day and the news
wasn't good. 'You've got a third-degree chemical burn,' he said to me so-
berly." Couture was scheduled for plastic surgery to repair his finger. His
case was severe, but many men who use poppers experience redness and

chafing because the liquid inevitably spills onto their nostrils when they inhale it.

Why? Why would a man want to inhale a caustic substance capable of causing severe chemical burns? Again the same response to this question: to enhance the sexual experience. Organic nitrites are used primarily to enhance sexual experience (other inhalants are used to alter mood). Poppers are rapid, short-acting vasodilators that allow gay men to be more relaxed and receptive during anal and oral sex. Other men report it increases their sexual arousal.

Recreational use of poppers is common for gay men and by itself does not indicate a substance abuse problem. It is not clear if users can become physically dependent on poppers, but without a doubt, many gay men can't engage in sexual activity without using them. For these men, no poppers equals no sex. If you use the criteria I developed for gay men and substance abuse, the inability to engage in sexual activity without substance use indicates a drug abuse problem.

## Sexual Addictions

A sexual addiction is a sexually related behavior that causes problems in one's life and which one is no longer able to control. Such sexual behaviors cover a wide spectrum and include compulsive masturbation, pornography, exhibitionism, use of prostitutes or paying for sex, anonymous sex, and voyeurism (to name only the most common). Engagement in more than one is the general rule.

Most insurance companies do not pay for treatment of the condition. When first introduced, many scoffed at the idea of sexual addictions, but over the intervening decades more and more evidence has amassed that, similar to other addictions, some people cannot control their sexual activities despite even severe consequences; their sexual activity has become compulsive.

Mario's situation poignantly illustrates this condition. Mario's addiction is Internet pornography. Often he would use methamphetamine so that his combined pornography and masturbation sessions—three to four times weekly—could last upwards of twelve hours. That's a lot of time spent on pornography, but this is not an uncommon scenario. Such compulsive behaviors can lead to many problems: relationship and

family turmoil, loss of relationships, loss of career opportunities, expo-
sures to sexually transmitted diseases, legal problems, and even suicide
attempts. On his web site, Patrick Carnes, the foremost researcher on sexual addiction, offers a screening for sexual addiction. (See www.sexhelp
.com for more information.)

Today, more and more gay men are recognized as having a sexual
addiction, often—but not always—in combination with substance use. To
learn more about gay men dealing with sexual addiction, see *Cruise Control,* an excellent self-help book written by Robert Weiss, director of the
Sexual Recovery Institute in Los Angeles and an expert on sexual addictions in the gay male community.[12]

::

Gay men can have substance abuse problems that do not involve sexual
activity. For example, some men I have worked with use drugs to cover
up the loneliness and emptiness stemming from the shame in their lives;
sexual activity is not a priority. Still, it is the rare gay male addict whose
sexual activity is not somehow affected by substance use, and vice versa.
And though this chapter spotlighted a subset of drugs most notorious for
their role in sexual activity, all drugs of abuse have the same potential.
Alcohol and crack cocaine, in particular, are well known for their effects
on sexual arousal and performance. Addressing drug use and gay men
also means paying attention to the "party and play" aspect of gay male
social and sexual interaction.

## CHAPTER THREE

# SHAME

SHAME DOES NOT CAUSE ADDICTION IN GAY MEN. As we've already discussed, addiction is a brain disease caused by long-term chemical and structural changes in the brain resulting from repeated drug abuse. However, shame often gives rise to substance use and contributes to ongoing abuse. When a gay man seems unable to maintain abstinence despite sincere efforts, shame may be an underlying factor. If left unexplored, feelings of shame may prevent a gay man from dealing with substance use problems or finding joy and meaning in life.

A pivotal moment in my career occurred two decades ago when I began working with Khalil; my session with his "family" became an epiphany in my understanding of the complexities facing gay men in recovery. Khalil was twenty-seven when he sought substance abuse treatment services at the outpatient agency where I worked. I'm sure he wasn't impressed with me since I was several years younger than him and had very limited experience in addictions treatment. Still, during the first month of weekly sessions, he revealed his sexual orientation. I wasn't too surprised since he appeared to be a very effeminate man, and at that point I associated effeminacy with sexual orientation (which we now know is certainly not true). He told me he was in a relationship of four years' duration and asked if he could bring in his partner so that I could answer some of his questions.

Other than his partner and an older man (whom I suspected was a former lover), Khalil said he had no family. He had left home as a teenager and moved to the city; he had lived on the street, prostituted himself, and started using heroin when he was eighteen. He had had no contact with his family of origin in almost a decade, and his friendships in Philadelphia were superficial. I decided to invite Khalil's partner and the older confidant into a session to "consult" on his case. I would answer their questions and learn about some of the concerns and risks they perceived for Khalil.

On the day of our session, Khalil's concerned others were more than engaging; they revealed issues and concerns that had not yet arisen in our sessions (much to his consternation). They described his risk factors, triggers, and their previous attempts at helping him to stop using. Overall, the session was going smoothly, and I was quite proud of the progress that was being made. Toward the ending of our hour together, I asked the question that would forever transform my understanding of gay men in recovery.

"You've given me a lot of information today, and I think this will be very beneficial in planning Khalil's treatment," I began. "But one topic we haven't discussed is his sexual orientation. How do you think his being gay affected his drug use? How do you think it will impact his recovery?"

The three of them looked at me as if I was a fool, as if I had asked a question that had an obvious answer.

"Well of course it would be easier if he wasn't gay," replied the older confidant after a few moments of complete—and uncomfortable— silence. "But that is a struggle that we must all go through. I'm sure my life would have been very different if I wasn't attracted to men."

Thankfully I didn't have another client scheduled after Khalil's session, since this comment led to an hour of dialogue that benefited me much more than it did them. All three men—Khalil, his current lover, and the older "friend"—were deeply and profoundly ashamed of their sexual orientation. The older man had had an alcohol problem years ago but recovered through AA; later, he had attended a self-help group for gay men that attempted to change their sexual orientation via support and prayer. This had not worked for him, and he had been celibate for at least five years. Both Khalil and his partner, despite confirming their love and commitment for each other, agreed that if a remedy for homosexuality were available, they would take it without hesitation. These two men were Khalil's support system, the people he turned to when he was in crisis or simply needed to talk, yet both experienced the same shame when it came to sexual orientation. The older man in particular was not only educated but seemed wise, yet he opted to forgo his sexuality rather than to live a life of covert shame.

Gay men must address—in one way or another—their sexual orientation during treatment for substance abuse. Many family members are deeply uncomfortable with this component of recovery. They'll address every other issue but this one. Family members may be gay themselves and may be uncomfortable with their sexuality. Some may support or have even personally tried reparative therapy—a "treatment" designed to make gay men and women straight, based on the belief that homosexuality is wrong, a sin, and an aberration, and that gay people simply cannot live fulfilling lives.

Helping professionals will see these beliefs in family members who subtly hint, or even demand, that their loved one should try to become straight in order to rectify his life and end his struggles with substance use; if he doesn't, he will drop further into drug use.

Such family members can help their loved one to a limited degree, and their efforts might even be outright damaging. He is a gay man and this will not change. No amount of reparative therapy, prayer, and strenuous effort on their or his part will change this. Making a demand for that to be different can put an unnecessary barrier in a newly recovering gay man's path.

## SHAMELESS GAY MEN

As I read the research, interview professionals who work with gay men with substance abuse problems, and visit facilities that treat them, I repeatedly hear the words "internalized homophobia" and "shame." Many in the field contend that these two experiences are at the root of gay male substance abuse and believe that if we could only "cure" gay men of these two internal states, we would dramatically reduce, if not outright eliminate, alcohol and drug abuse in the gay male community. According to this view, substance abuse is merely a symptom of deeper sexual identity concerns.

Obviously, not every gay man has shame underlying his substance use. Though early research found a correlation, these studies were few in number, had too few participants to generalize to the entire gay male population, and used questionable research methods. More recent studies indicate that gay men often use drugs and alcohol as part of adopting a gay lifestyle, one that involves socializing in bars and clubs. Some men are consumed by this lifestyle, and substance use problems inevitably arise for some (but most certainly not the majority). So let's dispel the belief that if a gay man has a substance use problem, he must also be ashamed of his sexual orientation. As two examples, let me introduce you to Daniel and Marcel.

## Daniel

Twenty-eight-year-old Daniel describes himself as a "rebel." He dropped out of school in tenth grade and at the age of sixteen ran away from home to begin his grand journey across the continent, including stays in Mexico and Canada. If asked, he will share details of his adventures, but first he has to sit still long enough for such a dialogue to occur. He is physically restless and constantly squirming about in his chair. His mind races at warp speed, rarely slowing down unless he is using sedative-type drugs. Daniel cannot tolerate boredom; he thrives on excitement and sensation. The more intense the experience, the more rewarding and stimulating he finds it.

Not surprisingly, Daniel has had sexual contact with many people in many different ways. Indeed, his entire cross-country journey was funded by prostitution. He starred in one gay porn film, was a male stripper, allowed himself to be urinated and defecated on by males with these kinks, worked as a (unqualified) lifeguard at a nudist resort, and was even held prisoner for two days locked in a makeshift dungeon by a bondage-and-discipline practitioner coming down off a methamphetamine binge. He has had sex with men and women, solo and in groups, in private and public. He absolutely prefers males to females, but if he is horny enough, any available and willing person will do.

With such a history, it should also come as no surprise that Daniel is willing to experiment with any and every drug. If you name it, he has tried it at least once. His preference is for those substances that help mellow him. He will argue you to exhaustion that he is not ashamed of his sexuality; while he has learned that it is sometimes safer not to "flaunt" one's sexual orientation in certain circumstances, he does not equate this self-protective stance with shame or internalized heterosexism. He has no interest in working on shame issues and looks aghast at the mere mention of such an approach. He recognizes his low tolerance for boredom and his risk-taking personality as the real cause for intervention. Now almost thirty, he has little to show for his lifetime of adventure. He has no money, no high school diploma, has burned through friends and family, and is using several hundred dollars' worth of drugs weekly, which he funds through sexual activity. He really isn't sure whether he wants to stop using drugs entirely, but he can no longer hide from his fears for the future.

## Marcel

Marcel, age twenty-seven, was raised in a rural area by a family that strictly forbid alcohol use. Throughout his adolescence he never once smoked a cigarette, drank a beer, or experimented with any other type of drug use. When he received a job offer in Philadelphia after college, he was delighted. He had never had the opportunity to explore his true sexuality during his adolescence and had instead dated several females in order to fit in with his peers. But he knew he was attracted to males, and a big urban environment seemed to be the perfect place to hook up with other gay men. And this he did with abandon. At the age of twenty-two, he entered his first gay bar and was instantly terrified. He could feel people sizing him up, and it didn't take long for someone to offer him a drink. Two drinks later he was intoxicated and leaving for the apartment of a stranger for the first gay sexual experience of his life; it was terrifying, enthralling, and wondrous. He returned to the bar the very next night. And the night after that. Soon he was experimenting with sex in ways that he had even dreamed about during adolescence. He found two bars he really liked, and he became "a regular" with an established group of other gay men. They would meet three or four nights a week to dance, drink, party, and often have some type of sexual activity. Marcel does not hesitate to recall this period in his life as a time of voluntary reckless abandonment. He was introduced to cocaine, poppers, marijuana, and Ecstasy. And he believes he would have continued in this lifestyle for much longer had he not contracted a curable sexually transmitted disease; this was an immediate wake-up call. The combination of the STD and the staggering amount of money he spent partying made him realize that this lifestyle could not last. As for shame, Marcel laughs at the notion. He attributed his substance abuse to his naïveté and the bedazzlement of big-city gay life, not to self-hatred for his identity.

There are many reasons people begin using substances, including to perform better, to feel good, curiosity, and peer pressure. Many gay men who develop a substance use problem recognize that they are headed for trouble and either decrease or stop using their own. Other gay men, however, cannot do this, and it is often these men who are struggling with shame issues. When I work with a gay man who repeatedly fails at his recovery efforts, I assume that shame is somewhere in the picture.

## OUR SHAMING SOCIETY

The U.S. Substance Abuse and Mental Health Services Administration (SAMHSA) states that "Internalized homophobia is a key concept in understanding issues facing gay men" in substance abuse treatment.[1] *Accepting Ourselves and Others,* a substance abuse self-help book written specifically for GLBT individuals, devotes an entire chapter to homophobia, particularly internalized homophobia. The authors of *Accepting Ourselves and Others* note that, when inventorying their personal strengths and weaknesses, most gay men in treatment list homosexuality as their number one character defect.[2]

## INTERNALIZED HOMOPHOBIA

A 2004 study that examined the predictors of substance abuse among gay youth found that they experience stigmatization in society leading to victimization, rejection, and other stressful events not encountered by straight men and women.[3] Many professionals believe these factors contribute to gay male substance abuse. The researcher of the study suggested that instead of using the term "internalized homophobia" we consider "internalized heterosexism." After all, the entire word "phobia" does not accurately describe the experience of homophobia, since it not a really a phobia, or a fear, but rather a prejudice based on heterosexual norms.

Internalized homophobia (or internalized heterosexism) often leads to feelings of shame. If you experience the former, then many believe it impossible not to develop the latter. Brené Brown, a professor at the University of Houston and author of several books on shame, has spent almost a decade studying the topic, and she defines shame as an intensely painful belief that one is flawed and unworthy of love and belonging. And since it is impossible for any gay man to have lived a life without experiencing heterosexism, *the conclusion is that all gay men have shame to some degree.* Too many men believe that they are not only unlovable but even unworthy of love.

Sylvia Kay Fisher, a research psychologist at the Bureau of Labor Statistics and a former therapist who has worked extensively with gay and lesbian clients, developed a checklist of the reasons gay men engage in alcohol use, but it is just as useful for all forms of substance use. One section of the inventory scrutinizes internalized homophobia/heterosexism within the gay man himself and another section poses questions about the societal homophobia he has experienced.

Take a minute to review the list on the next page. Can you imagine going through life recognizing not only that self-hatred and shame are the primary emotions of your daily life but also that family, friends, religions, and even society as a whole have little tolerance for you? How many gay men must hide their identity, possibly leading a second life, in order to protect their jobs and sometimes even their personal safety due to the hatred and ill will of so many people? Is it any wonder that so many gay men find relief for their pain in drug use and that even after several months of abstinence, the effort of carrying this burden becomes too much to bear without the assistance found in mind-altering substances?

I counsel gay men who experience internalized heterosexism and shame and who believe they are unlovable. I counsel middle-aged men who have never been in a meaningful relationship and instead meet their human need for intimacy with endless sexual (and frequently anonymous) escapades. I know men—professionally and personally—who would convert to heterosexuality if it were only possible. Heterosexism and internalized homophobia are strong underlying factors in why so many gay men develop substance abuse problems. Let me introduce you to two men for whom this is true.

## Justin

Justin is thirty-one and recently approached his primary care doctor to write a prescription for Revia (naltrexone), a medication that decreases cravings for alcohol. After sixteen years of increasing alcohol use, he now wanted to stop completely. His boss had just threatened to write him up for any more absences, and Justin did not want to risk losing his job. He had missed so many days due to hangovers that he no longer had any remaining sick time. Two years ago, he had begun to suspect that he had an alcohol problem, and when he confided in one of his female friends, she recommended that he try an Alcoholics Anonymous meeting. He cringed at that idea and instead tried to stop on his own. And he was successful,

## THE CONNECTIONS BETWEEN
## HOMOPHOBIA AND DRUG ABUSE

The following checklist, developed by Sylvia Kay Fisher, identifies some of the most common stressors that lead reasons gay men (and all sexual minorities) to turn to alcohol and other drug use.

### INTERNALIZED HOMOPHOBIA

☐   1. I drink because I am ashamed of being gay/lesbian.

☐   2. I drink because I feel guilty that I am gay/lesbian.

☐   3. I drink because I am disappointed in myself and my orientation.

☐   4. I drink when I am depressed about my life and the direction it's going.

☐   5. I drink when I want to forget how much I hate myself.

☐   6. I drink because I cope better with being gay/lesbian when I have a good buzz on.

☐   7. I drink because I see no reason not to drink; after all, life for gays and lesbians is one painful event after another.

### HOMOPHOBIA FROM OTHERS

☐   8. I drink because I am afraid to come out to members of my family.

☐   9. I drink because most of my so-called friends don't know I am a gay/lesbian.

☐ 10. I drink to forget I am a gay/lesbian in a straight world.

☐ 11. I drink because I can't trust my friends to accept me for who I really am.

☐ 12. I drink because I know my parents are ashamed of me for being gay/lesbian.

☐ 13. I drink because my religion teaches me that I am unworthy and unacceptable.

☐ 14. I drink because I feel like the whole world is judging me.

☐ 15. I drink because of the strain of being in the closet at work.

☐ 16. I drink so I'll care less about what people think of me.

☐ 17. I drink because I resent the way society treats gays/lesbians.

☐ 18. I drink because I get tired of people spreading gossip and rumors about my sexual orientation.

☐ 19. I drink because my parents reject me for being gay/lesbian.

☐ 20. I drink because I am afraid that someone will physically assault me because I am gay/lesbian.[4]

at least for several weeks at a time. At one point, he even managed to stay alcohol free for nearly three months. But finally, with great embarrassment, he attended two AA meetings—and quickly realized he did not like them. He couldn't accept the principle of "turning one's will over to a Higher Power" and was embarrassed to introduce himself as an "alcoholic." Was he an alcoholic? He didn't think so, although he did recognize that alcohol use was causing problems in his life.

His doctor agreed to write the prescription for Revia but said that the medication alone would likely be inadequate and that medication works best with counseling. However, going to counseling was the last thing that Justin wanted to do. He knew that if he sought help and tried to make genuine progress, he would have to be honest about himself. The "issue" Justin was hoping to avoid was this: He was sexually attracted to males.

Justin had learned early in life that homosexuality was "wrong," "disgusting," and, from the perspective of his parents, "evil." Being called "gay" and "faggot" in the schoolyard were the most threatening insults hurled back and forth between males during his childhood. Growing up, he was careful to hide his attraction to other males. He dated and even had sex with females several times in his life, though he found neither activity particularly enjoyable. During his last year of high school, he had his first sexual experience with another male, a teammate from his soccer club. Justin quit the team several weeks later, without explanation to his perplexed and disappointed teammates and parents. He spent many years masturbating to images of males in physical fitness magazines; he clearly remembered the hormonal explosion that occurred when he discovered a cache of *Playgirl* magazines in his neighbor's recycling bin. Now, ten years later, he still treasured these discoveries and kept them well hidden.

Justin has no friends who are gay. He is mortified that his repertoire of sexual activity consists primarily of masturbation and anonymous sex. In his mid-twenties he found an adult video store with private screening booths concealed behind a turnstile and locked door; now several times a month (but only after dark) he visits this store and receives quick oral sex from other men in the booths (all of them ignore the overhanging signs prohibiting more than one person in a booth at a time). He exits the store immediately afterward; he has never once said a word to any male he meets here. There are no "hellos" or "good-byes" in this setting.

Justin has no doubt he is gay and makes no pretense that he is bisexual, since he has no sexual arousal to females. He is disgusted, miserable, and angry with himself for being this way. If there were a way for him to change his sexual orientation, he would. Indeed, he even contemplated reparation therapy but doubted the technique's validity. So this is his life: unhappy and profoundly ashamed. Justin knows that he drinks to numb these feelings and his life in general. And since he has never told anyone in his life that he is gay (though of course he suspects that some people already know), he is alone. Sometimes—now more often than in the past— he wishes he were dead. Although he could never kill himself, he wouldn't put up a fight to stay alive. If this is the remainder of life—loneliness, self-hate, quick blow jobs by strangers in dark booths with sticky floors and that smell of sweat—he would rather die. His doctor had no idea how seemingly insurmountable that task was when he recommended counseling to Justin. He is dying internally, not from his sexual orientation, but from the resulting deep shame that is destroying his very being.

## Steven

Lest readers think that all men whose lives are wracked by shame and internalized homophobia are "closet cases" who lead socially isolated lives and dread the thought that their secret desires may be publicly revealed, let me introduce you to Steven. I worked with him in an inpatient setting, and from the very first report I had about him from the weekend staff, I had to respect his stance. He was admitted on a Saturday, and that very same night he complained to the staff that some other patients were using derogatory comments such as "faggot" in their general conversation; he didn't believe these comments were directed at him but still thought the recovery environment was less safe and welcoming than it could be. He even volunteered to share his concern in the Sunday morning community meeting. And that he did. He told the assembled twenty men and women that he was gay and that he expected and outright demanded respectful treatment. Later two other patients—a lesbian and a gay man— privately pulled him aside and thanked him for his fearlessness in addressing an issue that they had felt powerless to influence; they were certainly not going to "out" themselves.

Upon hearing this Monday morning, I was excited to meet Steven. Behind closed doors, however, I encountered a far less stalwart figure. He had not spoken to his parents or younger brother for almost five years; he believed his sexuality had driven an insurmountable wedge between them. He had had a series of disastrous relationships, and he admitted that while he was without doubt gay, he despised gay sex. He had never had any sexual contact with another male without being drunk or high and now considered himself "asexual," since he hadn't engaged in any sexual contact for more than two years. While Steven demanded respect, he hated his sexuality and would have consented to any procedure that would make him straight if one had only been available. Every weekend found him bouncing from gay bar to gay bar; he was known as a "man who knows how to party." Still, in spite of his bravado in disclosing his sexual orientation without hesitation, Steven was a conflicted rebel who hated himself and his life; although he wasn't in the least bit worried that other people knew his sexual orientation, he lived in terror that they might recognize his own self-hatred for being gay.

## FORMS OF SHAME

Often, gay male substance abusers must cope with two (or more) forms of shame. First, many experience shame due to their sexual identity. Almost all gay men report that they knew they were different from their peers at even an early age. Even when their understanding of sexuality was quite limited, boys who mature into gay men inherently understand that they are unlike their male friends. Most parents, of course, assume that their children are heterosexual. And so these youth, who are all too eager to please their parents and other adults in their lives, learn to disconnect from their true selves. As adolescents they work hard to hide any difference in order to fit in; such defenses may continue to develop well into adulthood. As Robert P. Cabaj describes in the *Journal of Gay and Lesbian Psychotherapy:*

> When adolescents who have disconnected themselves from any awareness of their homosexual feelings begin to recognize the source of their sense of difference, they may work even harder to suppress these feelings by isolating themselves and avoiding situations that may stir up their longings. Some of these youth may devote extraordinary energy to academic or career success to cover up their underlying shame

and sense of being defective; others may become depressed, isolated, guarded, and lonely, expecting to be rejected and ignored if their true feelings were revealed.[5]

As the above quote indicates, even the most outwardly successful man can hold profound shame regarding his sexual orientation. And for men from certain ethnic communities, identifying oneself as gay may be particularly stigmatizing.

In addition to shame over one's sexuality, most gay male substance abusers also experience shame over their drug use. They have likely hurt and disappointed others, lied, stolen, and even introduced others to substance use. By the time people recognize that they have a problem with substances and their lives have become unmanageable, many friends and family have already pulled away from them, and they have lost the respect of important people in their lives. Add to this financial, legal, and employment problems, and it is no wonder substance abusers are ashamed of themselves and reluctant to face the people who would otherwise be their primary supports.

Finally, the gay community can itself be shaming. While many assume that, as a long-standing stigmatized group, the gay community would be welcoming and supportive, there is little evidence to support this conclusion. The gay community has always struggled with current issues of diversity—such as the divide between black and white, between black and Latino, between gays in general and the transgendered community, between gays and bisexuals, and between those with HIV and those without. In general, it has not demonstrated an attitude of inclusiveness to those who do not fit its narrow definition of "gay."

Indeed, many see the "gay community" as limited to the urban gay white male or female. It has only been in the last fifteen years or so that the boundaries of this definition have loosened to permit a vocal African American presence. This is, of course, not to say that African American gays and lesbians did not exist up until this point but rather that their presence was too often marginalized. Other gay demographic groups are not only marginalized—their existence is almost unknown. For example, do we know of any gay Filipinos, Mexicans, Vietnamese, Koreans, Cubans, and American Indians in our own communities? How about gay senior citizens? How about those who the gay community deems unattractive?

Imagine living as a gay man who not only dislikes himself due to his sexuality but who also encounters the hostility from society in general and sometimes the very people he loves the most. This individual cannot even find refuge in the gay community itself. Is it any wonder then that he turns to drugs to find solace and that stopping is so challenging?

::

Again, not every man with a significant substance abuse problem is plagued by internalized heterosexism. However, in my experience and that of every professional I interviewed for this book, these feelings are overwhelmingly evident in most gay men we treat. Indeed, everyone internalizes heterosexism to a certain degree since we are all raised in a straight world. Although most gay men leap over this hurdle and move on with their lives, others find it impossible to take such a leap. Instead, they turn to drugs and alcohol, obliterate their senses through sexual activity, attempt to pass as straight, or, most tragically, end their own lives.

If a man seems unable to achieve abstinence or continually falters after promising beginnings, internalized heterosexism could well be at play. In such cases, counseling efforts should focus on his feelings of shame. Most counselors will address the following topics in one form or another:

- feelings of heterosexism

- relationships and sexual behaviors

- coming-out issues

- self-acceptance

As he learns to trust and be increasingly honest in his counseling relationship, he may experience complete acceptance by another person for the first time in his life. If you are a helping professional who has had a similar experience with a gay client, you know that such an experience is transformative for him. This one relationship can become the catalyst for incredible positive momentum. Most often family members and concerned others cannot offer this same unconstrained acceptance, one that comes with "no strings attached." Yet his connection with even one completely accepting person will ultimately touch all of his relationships. The change may be slow, but it will come. And while he is working on his own internalized heterosexism, it is also the time to be working on your own.

::

## CHAPTER FOUR

# THE ROLE OF
# CONCERNED OTHERS

THIS CHAPTER IS FOR family members, lovers, and others who are concerned about a gay man suffering from alcohol or other drug abuse. Here we'll address what you can do to help in this time of crisis.

Several months ago I attended an education session for families with loved ones who were in inpatient addiction treatment. For half an hour the presenter gave a warm, concise, and extremely professional overview of the latest research on addiction; she touched on genetics, state-of-the-art brain research, co-occurring conditions, and personality characteristics associated with substance abuse. As she concluded, she asked the audience if they had any questions. For a few uncomfortable seconds the group sat silent, evidently still processing the information they had just heard. Soon, however, one woman raised her hand.

"Thank you for that fascinating presentation," she said sheepishly, almost as if she were uncomfortable continuing her comments. "But our son is being released from your facility next week, and my husband and I really need to know what to do. How do we work with him when he comes home?"

The question seemed to resonate with the audience, as family members starting whispering to each other and nodding their heads in agreement. All of the other topics—the genetics, the brain research, co-occurring conditions, and personality characteristics associated with addiction—might be fascinating, and at another time and place even very beneficial to understand, but these were families struggling with immediate crises.

One person in their family had brought turmoil into their lives, and more than anything, they needed directions on how to survive as a family when their loved one returned home. They desperately needed pragmatic and detailed advice on what to do and say that would be helpful.

Because so many gay men have biological families that minimize and even completely cut off contact due to sexuality, many create their own families wholesale from available peer networks. They craft a constellation of individuals who stand in for siblings and parents, many with a depth of attachment, concern, loyalty, and love that equals if not supersedes that of the gay man's biological family. Although this may not match the definition of "family" as defined in a standard dictionary, it nonetheless comprises the true family of the substance abuser in question.

Perhaps this is your first experience dealing with substance abuse issues. Or maybe you're in recovery yourself or have firsthand experience from helping another family member or friend. Maybe you have seen people succeed the first time they attempted to stop using (it does happen far more often than is acknowledged), or perhaps you have witnessed somebody enter treatment repeatedly, each time with the highest of hopes and aspirations, only to relapse when the formal treatment ended. Tragically, you may have witnessed loved ones die directly from their substance use (such as a car accident while intoxicated or an overdose) or through the slow accumulation of physical damage from years of drug use. You may be approaching the task of helping this loved one with a sense of anticipation, dread, and even hopelessness, particularly if he has failed at past attempts to quit. You will fall somewhere on a continuum between knowing much about substance use recovery and knowing nothing at all. But, regardless of your own experiences, beliefs, and hopes for the substance user, remember that the man for whom you are seeking help will forge his own recovery route.

There is no one right way to achieve recovery from substance use. Recently the National Institute on Drug Abuse, the premier research institution in the world for substance abuse treatment, compiled a list of thirteen core principles of drug addiction treatment. Strikingly, it proclaims that "No single treatment is appropriate for everyone."[1]

Let me repeat that: *There is no singular right way of coping with substance abuse*; it is up to each man to establish his own path. Some of this work will be similar for anyone coping with substance abuse, while other tasks are specific to gay men. And some paths to recovery are right only for a particular individual. What you can do is urge and, if necessary, demand that your loved one seek help using both traditional interventions and state-of-the-art research. He will need that help to create a recovery plan that will support him when the once seemingly clear path becomes suddenly clouded.

## THE ROLE OF THE FAMILY

A man abusing drugs and/or alcohol may be able to hide his problem from an employer and even friends for years; it is almost always the family who is the first to notice a problem. Still, in the not-too-distant past, the role of the family in substance abuse recovery was fairly insignificant; family members were coached to avoid enabling behaviors and to attend Al-Anon or another self-help group for spouses and families of alcoholics and drug addicts. Recovery was seen as a quest that could only be pursued by the addict with assistance from peers in recovery and possibly a counselor or therapist. Families were told that they were powerless to influence a loved one's substance use and they were expected to stand on the sidelines and simply watch the ups and downs of the recovery process. They were also taught how to protect themselves from the ravages of their loved one's addiction. Times have changed. Studies now show that actively involving the family significantly improves treatment outcomes. Additionally, state-of-the-art research finds value in including not only spouses, partners, and biological family members, but a network of individuals who play an important role in a substance abuser's life—including friends, co-workers, neighbors, and anyone else who has a long-standing and positive relationship with the abuser and who is invested in his recovery.[2] As it stands, some form of engagement by significant concerned others is now considered the standard of care for drug and alcohol abuse treatment.

Loved ones *can* help a man whose life is careening out of control due to his substance use. Indeed, the most common reason a person with a substance use problem initially seeks help is due to pressure from family members, partners, and close friends. The only other motivating factor that even comes close is compulsory treatment by the legal system. If both the family and the legal system are mandating treatment, the odds for recovery are even better. Forget that antiquated advice that says a person must be intrinsically motivated to find success in recovery; research now proves that mandated and/or coerced treatment can lead to successful outcomes just as often as voluntary interventions.[3]

It would be nice to believe that the person having problems recognizes and is concerned about how his substance abuse is hurting himself and others, but he may either be blind to these consequences or unable to stop despite wanting to. The active involvement of friends, family, and concerned others can help the abuser recognize the severity of his abuse and lead him to seek out some form of treatment, stay with it, and avoid relapse.

That said, there are times when he will need to separate from family and friends, and instead turn to counselors, helping professionals, and fellow recovering people for his support. You might feel more involved if your loved one came to you with his worries and problems, but depending on the history and amount of negative emotion that accrued in your relationship, such fears and revelations may be best discussed with a counselor or another Twelve Step member, at least in the beginning. In time, intimate sharing will return to your own relationship.

## THE GOOD NEWS FOR LOVED ONES

- You can make a positive difference in another person's recovery.

- If negative feelings, long-standing grudges, and animosity have developed between you and your loved one who is abusing substances (common in such situations), these wounds can heal in recovery. Yes, your relationship can improve.

- You can work toward improving your own life regardless of what happens with your loved one. Sometimes even the man most resistant to change will suddenly seek out recovery when he recognizes that others are moving on in their lives.

- Finally, sometimes you simply have to give up, at least temporarily. If despite your continual efforts to help your loved one, both his life and your own life are spiraling hopelessly downward, it may be time to say "enough." Some men will not change or are not yet ready to change. Although it can be difficult to let go, doing so can be a relief.

## ABSTINENCE

In 2001 the U.S. Department of Health and Human Services released an addictions treatment guide for lesbian, gay, bisexual, and transgender individuals.[4] The manual listed numerous issues that sexual minorities must deal with in treatment, ranging from coming-out issues, internalized homophobia, lack of support, and histories of rejection, violence, and trauma. All of these issues (and so many more) need to be addressed in order for substance abuse issues to resolve. The first priority, however, is achieving abstinence. He can keep the cigarettes (if he must) and prescription medications that are used *only as prescribed*. Even if his drug of choice is marijuana and he uses alcohol only recreationally, complete abstinence from all mood-altering drugs is critical for at least the first several months. William Miller and Kathleen Carroll, renowned addiction experts, reviewed the science of addiction and found that an initial period of abstinence is invaluable for those with substance abuse problems.[5]

Why several months of abstinence at the very least?

• To give the brain and body an opportunity to heal.

• To monitor how difficult it is to stop all substance use. Maybe it will be quite easy, or maybe it won't. Don't be surprised if he actually fails at several months of abstinence; this proves just how much his substance use supersedes his willpower.

• To contemplate the advantages and disadvantages of substance use in his life and the lives of those who care about him.

• To give him the time and opportunity to take advantage of the education and support available in recovery. This could mean detox, inpatient or outpatient treatment, counseling, Twelve Step support groups, or any other kind of support that helps him see the benefits of a sober lifestyle.

Let's be clear: He is not making a commitment for life, and I realize that many gay men will not accept a lifestyle that does not offer at least occasional drug and alcohol experiences. Furthermore, feeling ambivalent about giving up substance use is natural and to be expected. Your loved one may even forgo three months of substance use simply to prove to you (and other concerned loved ones) that he really doesn't have a problem. "Look," he'll exclaim at the end of the successful trial period. "I told you I didn't have a drug problem. Now get off my back about my drug use." Even if he has no intention of long-term recovery and fully intends to resume substance use in the future after a hiatus or "rest" in which he has made some improvements in his life, he needs to stop for a time. At the end of at least three months of abstinence, he is in a better position to decide on the role drugs and alcohol will play in his life. After a period of abstinence, some men may realize that quitting drugs and alcohol is not a top priority right now and will return to their use. They may even give up before three months. Maybe they really don't have a problem. Maybe they do, but they're not ready for change. And maybe they'll try again in the future (or maybe not).

Other men, after a short period of abstinence, will try to use substances with moderation and be recreational users. Success with this depends as much on the makeup of each man as it does on his choice of drugs and alcohol; methamphetamine, for example, the drug currently ravaging the gay male community, is almost impossible to use in moderation. Still, I've worked in this field long enough to accept that most men will try to moderate their use regardless of what I and other treatment professionals suggest.

Another group of men may decide that long-term abstinence is in their best interest. With brains less clouded by substance use, they may now recognize the repercussions of drug abuse on their lives and those of their loved ones. They may find three months of abstinence more challenging and excruciating than they would have predicted; this serves as a wake-up call about the true nature of their problem. Their goal is to stop all drug and alcohol use.

Some men already know they have a substance use problem; they don't need a trial period of abstinence to evaluate the severity of their problem. Even so, the first step is still abstinence.

Early abstinence may not be the most pleasant, particularly if he has been abusing substances for a long time. It is extremely difficult for people who are accustomed to medicating their fears, worries, and uncertainties about life with substances to voluntarily give up something that brings pleasure or relief to them. But they must start somewhere, and this starting point is abstinence.

## WHEN DO CONCERNED OTHERS INTERVENE?

We once thought that an addict had to hit bottom before he could begin a sincere recovery effort. Families were thus scolded for "enabling," or protecting, an addict from the consequences of his addiction. The quicker he hit bottom, the quicker he would begin his recovery. We now know that "hitting bottom" is not necessary, and such a delay could lead to irreparable damage. The definition of "hitting bottom" was also different for every person; for some folks it might mean death or devastation beyond repair. We have since learned that it is far better if we can help stop this from happening in the first place.

If his substance use has become out of control, if it has progressed beyond recreational use, and/or its consequences otherwise warrant attention, it is the right time for concerned others to take action. As a concerned other, in the past you may have watched silently, or you may have been more than vocal in your concerns. Either way, your approach has not been successful. If you haven't stated your worries, if you have stood by silently while your fear, resentment, and frustration grew, the first intervention is to calmly express your concerns. He needs to hear this from you. Remaining silent on the topic allows him to delay acknowledging the severity of his problem. *So the first step is to express your fears and tell him you want him to get professional help for his substance use.*

Addiction professionals use extensive questionnaires and interviews to determine the likelihood of a substance use disorder. Family members and loved ones do not have these resources but can still determine whether a problem exists by asking just a few simple questions. A "yes" to any is a warning sign, but a positive response to two or more indicates a substance abuse problem.

## INTERVENTIONS

If your loved one agrees to take a break from drug use and get some help, then you may be in a position to help him make some crucial decisions and put together a plan of action. Can he do this strictly on his own? Will he attend Twelve Step meetings? Would seeing a counselor benefit him? If so, what type of counselor? Does he need formal treatment, including a

## WHAT ARE THE INDICATORS OF DRUG ABUSE?

Has drug use affected your loved one's

- responsibilities at home (such as not paying bills)?
- responsibilities and performance at work (such as calling in sick to work; being unable to perform at work; missing classes at school)?
- personal relationships (such as canceling on friends)?
- financial status?

Has his substance use led to legal repercussions?

Does he have feelings of shame, regret, or embarrassment about what he does when he gets high or when he once again fails to maintain abstinence?

Does he continue to use even though he puts himself in physically dangerous situations? This includes risky sexual activity, driving while intoxicated, not taking HIV medications as prescribed, and going to unsafe parts of town.

Tweaker.org offers a list of warning signs for addiction. Answering "yes" to any one of these questions may indicate addiction.[6]

### TOLERANCE—YOUR BODY'S GOTTEN USED TO THE DRUG, SO THAT:

1. To get off, you need to do a lot more than you used to. A bump just isn't what it used to be.

2. You can do a quarter in one night when half that much used to send you to the moon.

3. Snorting used to do the trick. Then smoking it was the only way to go. Now shooting it is the only way you think you feel anything.

4. You use more and more just to avoid the crash.

5. You use more and more frequently.

6. More often than not, you wind up doing more speed than you intended.

*continues*

7. More often than not, you stay high for longer than you intended.

8. You have a persistent desire to control your use.

9. You have attempted stopping your use, and been unsuccessful.

10. You spend a lot of time consumed by the drug—either being high, getting it, or recovering from it.

11. You give up (or practically give up) important social, recreational, or work-related activities because of using.

12. You use even though you know you have a problem and/or that speed keeps bringing problems into your life.

detox and/or rehab? This chapter—and chapter 11, addressed to romantic partners—will guide you through the different options available for your loved one. Other chapters in the book will help you understand what the first weeks of his abstinence will be like, how his drugs have affected his health and psyche, and the challenges he will face further down the road.

What if he says "no" when you ask him to consider getting help? What if refuses to consider how his substance use has affected the people who love him? What if he says he will reduce his use but not stop altogether? Unfortunately this response is not uncommon, and it is then up to you to decide what your next move is. Remember that being coerced into treatment doesn't mean it will be unsuccessful. Even if he quits his drug use resentful and kicking and screaming, quitting is what really matters. But if he adamantly refuses, then you must consider some other interventions.

## The Family Intervention

One option is a formal intervention. There are several books available on family intervention, and these are excellent resources for those who may need to take this route. This section will offer a brief overview of family interventions, much of it based on the exceptional work of Jeff Jay and Debra Jay, authors of *Love First: A Family's Guide to Intervention*. Interested readers can get more information from their web site—www.lovefirst.net.

Typically, an intervention is held after you and other loved ones have individually expressed your concerns about substance use and yet the abuser does not make an attempt to change his behavior. An "intervention" is a formal meeting in which the substance user is confronted by a group of concerned individuals who take turns sharing their observations, concerns, and hopes for his future. He is told in no uncertain terms that he needs to seek help or risk tough-love ramifications from the family. They will no longer allow him to manipulate them or negatively impact their lives; they will move on one way or the other.

Television depictions of interventions often end with the abuser heading off to a formal inpatient treatment program; however, such a conclusion is not necessarily possible with even the best planning. Interventions are often emotionally draining experiences with overlapping loose ends and indeterminate outcomes. There are many dynamics that need to be considered in planning an intervention, particularly who to include. For example, having just one family member present who doubts the severity of the loved one's problem, who has a history of enabling, or who folds easily under pressure might jeopardize the intervention's success. This person might suddenly side with the abuser during the intervention rather than backing the group's effort. And all it takes is just one person to question the extent of the abuser's substance use for the entire intervention to transform from a supportive confrontation to a squabbling session.

What does happen after the intervention? Is the abuser immediately whisked off to a treatment facility? And if so, what about his daily responsibilities, especially his job? Some believe that the more time a person has between a formal intervention and starting treatment, the less likely he is to actually enter treatment. While this may indeed be true, attempting to sort out all of the details in advance (such as arranging for time off from his job, insurance, working through the admission process of a treatment facility) without assurance he will actually enter treatment can be overwhelming for the individuals organizing the intervention. And what if the abuser refuses to enter treatment and commit to recovery? Will all of the family members be able to keep up their tough-love approach as the abuser attempts to find the weakest link in the clan? Maintaining such an approach is critical to the success of the intervention, a feat that many people simply cannot perform.

Although interventions may be somewhat complex, most families can be successful with them. However, in certain circumstances families may want help from a professional. According to Jeff Jay, "If there are complicating issues, however, you may need the help of a professional. For example, if there is a history of violence, if there are concurrent mental health problems, if there is a history of failed treatment attempts, or if there have been threats or attempts at suicide. Generally, any complicating factor that makes the group uncomfortable may indicate the need for professional guidance. Having said that, most families are perfectly capable of carrying out a structured intervention on their own, if they have the time and ability to prepare carefully."[7]

According to the Jays, an ideal family intervention consists of these steps:

- Bring together three to eight people who are important to the substance abuser and are willing to learn how to help.

- Set up a planning meeting to discuss moving forward with the intervention.

- Choose a detail person.

- Choose a team chairperson.

- Discuss the importance of not alerting the abuser to the intervention plans.

- List ways you've tried to help him that may have enabled the addiction.

- Put in writing all the negative consequences caused by the addiction problem.

- Write a one- to two-page letter to the abuser.

- Read your letters to each other, editing out anger, blame, and judgment.

- Determine bottom lines, and write them down on a separate page.

- Test each other's willingness to follow through with the bottom lines.

- Identify financial resources for covering treatment costs.

- Evaluate treatment centers using the evaluation questions.

- Set a date, time, and place for the rehearsal and the intervention.

- Choose a treatment center, answer its pre-intake questions, and make an appointment for admission.

- Make airline reservations if the treatment center is out of state.

- Create a plan likely to guarantee the abuser's presence at the intervention.

- Identify objections he may use to avoid or postpone treatment; then formulate your answers.

- Pack a suitcase using the guidelines provided by the treatment staff.

- Determine who should drive the abuser from the intervention to treatment.

- Compile a list of all prescribed medications he is presently using.

- Rehearse the intervention.

- Decide where each person will sit, including the abuser.

- Discuss the order in which you'll read your letters.

- Find a discreet place to park your cars.

- Script the chairman's introduction and closing statement.

- Review objections and answers.

- Plan to arrive at the intervention location 30 minutes before the abuser is expected to be there.

- If the intervention is taking place at the abuser's home, arrive as a group.

- After the intervention, call the admissions staff and let them know whether or not he has agreed to treatment.

- Collect all letters and send them to his treatment counselor.

- Sign up for the Family Program.[8]

As seen in the above protocol, many family interventions make use of written letters read to the abuser. In the Jays' experience, letters are typically one to two pages in length, handwritten or double-spaced, and use the following format:

1. Introduction: Write a brief opening statement of love that specifically states the nature of your relationship with the substance abuser.

2. Love: This is the longest part of the letter. Do not bring up problems related to addiction in this part of the letter. Instead, give specific reasons why you love and care about the person, remembering times when you were proud of him, when he was there for you, fun times you experienced together, examples of his best character traits. This part of the letter must be sincere, avoiding empty flattery. If the addict's behavior has been difficult for a long time, remember back to better days.

3. Reframing: Shift from the love section to a discussion of the problem by stating your understanding of addiction as a genetic disease. Differentiate addiction from character and willpower issues. Talk about the need for professional treatment. If other people in your family have suffered from alcoholism, mention that it runs in the family.

4. Facts: Provide specific, firsthand examples of problems caused by alcohol or other drugs. Include consequences experienced by the alcoholic and by yourself. Don't use judgmental or angry language. Don't try to tell the addict what he was thinking. Instead, describe what you saw and how you felt. Let the facts speak for themselves. Be brief. One to three examples is sufficient, and don't dredge up ancient history unless there is a very good reason to do so.

5. Commitment: Make a personal commitment to stand by the alcoholic and help him in any way that is possible and appropriate.

6. Ask: This is a direct request that the alcoholic immediately accept the treatment program being offered. If the treatment center provides special programs that will be of interest to your loved one, have one member of the intervention team mention those programs in his or her letter.

7. Affirmation: End on a positive note, painting a positive picture
of the future. Give your loved one a reason to want to get sober.
Speak of ways the addict is important to you and others. Give him
a sense of purpose. Express faith in his ability to follow through
and succeed.

Allow thirty to forty-five minutes to write your letter. Some people
prefer to write their letter one day, then revise it the next. Take your time,
and write from the heart. During the intervention training, share letters
with each other. Read them aloud during the rehearsal.

Make necessary edits. Remove any language that could make the
alcoholic or addict angry or defensive. Rewrite your letters to incorporate changes. Don't just scribble out parts or add things in the margins.
Always use loving, nonjudgmental honesty when talking about the problem. Don't skimp on the love part of the letter. When your loved one goes
to treatment, deliver the letters to his counselor.[9]

The most desired outcome of an intervention is an immediate admission to a rehab (preceded by a detox if necessary). By the time a family
decides to hold a formal intervention, the loved one's substance abuse
has likely become dire. Outpatient treatment will not suffice.

## Detachment

Another option for dealing with your loved one's substance abuse is to
maintain your current relationship but make changes to increase your day-
to-day satisfaction and lower your stress level—regardless of what he does.
We are now in the realm of Al-Anon and associated groups. When family members initially recognize that a substance problem exists, they try
to help as much as possible. And just as often, the person's problem gets
worse rather than better and the family's resentment, frustration, and hopelessness grows. This is a no-win situation for all involved. As Nowinski and
Baker explain in *The Twelve-Step Facilitation Handbook: A Systematic
Approach to Early Recovery from Alcoholism and Addiction,* "As people
become addicted, the people around them are also inevitably affected. The
closer you are to an addict—the more you love and care about them—the
more you're likely to be affected. Out of concern, we often tend to take too
much responsibility for the alcoholic or addict we care about."[10]

The word "enabling" has fallen into disfavor with clinicians, as it tends to be perceived as a criticism of families and their interaction with a substance user. Still, the concept holds true: spouses and other family members often modify their behaviors, patterns, and interactions in order to cope with the substance abuse of one family member. While such actions promise survival on a day-to-day basis, they unintentionally promote and even reward continued substance use. This is not to cast blame on family members; caretaking for someone with a substance abuse problem or assuming some (or most) of his responsibilities may be necessary if the family is to continue moving forward. At the same time, the addict encourages (often subtly) these behaviors in his loved ones, since they minimize the repercussions of his abuse. These behaviors might include giving him money, making excuses for him, assuming his responsibilities, and cleaning up after him. All involved are locked in an unhealthy dance in which the drug user is the lead partner. Loved ones are unwillingly along for the ride, attempting to make the best of a tumultuous existence.

It's obvious that none of the above behaviors encourage a person to stop using drugs; in fact, they do just the opposite. Some may even reward drug use. If you, as a concerned other, nurse an abuser during a hangover and demonstrate your love and tenderness, this affection is rewarding his use, particularly if these are the only times you show warmth due to the gradual accumulation of resentment over his drug use. While your actions may certainly seem necessary—and so much more humane than leaving him unconscious on the bathroom floor—in the long run, they are not helping his recovery efforts. Often you are blind to the repercussions of your actions, but more often than not, at some level you probably recognize that these actions may be doing more harm than healing. It's likely that you're also furious that you have assumed a role in allowing his behavior to continue.

If you do recognize some of your enabling behaviors, go easy on yourself. Now is the time to stop, look at your actions, and ask yourself if what you are doing is hurting or helping the substance abuser. In the past, you may not have known how to intervene, short of ending the relationship. And of course, recipients of such caretaking actions do not complain. I've never once heard a man with a substance use problem complain that his spouse, partner, or friend was making it too easy for his drug use to continue. As Nowinski and Baker explain, "Every addict and alcoholic actively promotes and encourages enabling in those around them, since it is almost as important to their addiction as their source of liquor or drugs. Without his/her enablers, the alcoholic or addict would suffer many more negative consequences and hit bottom that much sooner."[11]

Al-Anon promotes the widely accepted stance of detachment—focusing on our own lives and allowing the substance user to take responsibility for his actions. It's *such* a simple concept but, oh so difficult to put into action. Detachment does not mean we stop loving the man with a substance use problem, nor do we stop feeling compassion. Instead we recognize that we have done all we could and the problem is no longer in our control. And instead of simply giving up on the relationship, we hold on to hope that the future will bring positive change.

For those who go this route, there are some basic tenets that need to be addressed. If you don't think you can follow these, detachment is not for you:

1. In spite of your love, you cannot change or control another adult. Love does not cure all.

2. Your diligence and willpower will come to naught if your loved one does not want to change. Al-Anon unequivocally reminds families that they did not cause the substance abuse problem, they cannot control it, and they cannot cure it.

3. If you believe that you must protect a loved one from the negative consequences in his life—that to not do so is unloving and even cruel—your attempt at detachment is doomed from the start.

Detachment means adopting a tough-love approach in which you allow your loved one to experience the consequences of his actions. Simultaneously, this is the time to focus on yourself and your needs; your attention is on improving your own life, always hoping that he will eventually choose to transform his life as well. You will no longer make excuses for his behavior (including calling to cancel for work and other important dates). You will no longer plead, beg, or cajole him to stop. You will no longer give him money. Words and feeble attempts on his part are no longer acceptable. You need to see a change in his behaviors.

## Despair and Hopelessness

The last option, the one I discourage, is to accept your lot as sharing a life with an addict and continuing on with minimal change. If you are the partner of an addict, you may be sharing the same home and possibly even raising children together. Other family members may not live with him but are still involved in his life. Whether you share the same home or live in separate states, to accept this option tells me more about you than it does your loved one who is actively abusing drugs and/or alcohol. For example, gay men with shame issues who believe they are unlovable will often cling to a destructive romantic relationship with a substance user no matter how severe the consequences. Others have more practical reasons: If one partner controls all of the family's money, leaving could be financially disastrous. Some loved ones never give up hope; they wait for the day their loved one will make a sudden and remarkable improvement. Although spontaneous remissions do occur—and far more frequently than clinical lore and Twelve Step groups acknowledge—it is also possible that it may never occur. How long do you allow your life to be a casualty of his drug use?

There isn't a research study out there that shows positive outcomes from remaining passive about a family member's substance abuse. The opposite is true: everybody suffers. As this chapter has pointed out, the most beneficial family responses are

- Communication: Families assertively ask their loved one to change and detail the consequences of continued drug use.

- Rearrange consequences: Family members purposefully increase the number of negative consequences their loved one will experience when he uses drugs and increase the positive consequences when he doesn't.

- Self-care: Family members take care of and protect themselves no matter what the drug user does.

If you decide to remain in a relationship with a man who refuses to acknowledge that he has a substance use problem or who will not even try to abstain from drugs for at least three months for the sake of your relationship, you should expect the quality of your life to continually erode. Your predicament will likely not improve, and it can get far worse.

## Using the Support and Guidance of Counselors

When you confront the man in your life who is having substance use problems, there is a very good chance that he will agree with you, particularly if he has recognized the complications his substance abuse is causing. He might stop his use then and there and never pick up again. If he needs extra support, he might go to a Twelve Step or related group. And if he needs even more help, he may decide to seek counseling. Obviously, the more severe the problem, the more help that both he and you will need. Any recovery plan can benefit from the addition of counseling and a support group.

According to Harold Urschel, author of *Healing the Addicted Brain*, counseling is essential for recovery but comes with risks:

> Whether you are wrestling with an addiction or you simply love some-
> one with this problem, the importance of getting good therapy cannot
> be overstated. Ideally, the individual, family, or group therapist that you
> work with will deal with your specific issues sensitively and skillfully.
> Unfortunately, even knowledgeable and experienced therapists may drop
> the ball at times, or simply not be a good fit. If this happens, please do
> not use the unsatisfactory experience as an excuse to drop out of therapy.
> Yes, bad therapy can be a miserable experience, dashing your hopes and
> wasting time and money. But good therapy is absolutely necessary! If it
> doesn't work with the first therapist, look for another.[12]

If your loved one does want to seek professional help, do some research to help him find a qualified counselor who will meet his needs. Don't assume that all are equal. There are great counselors. There are adequate counselors. And there are those who shouldn't be in the field. Thomas McLellan, deputy director of the Office of National Drug Control Policy and one of most recognized professionals in the field of addiction medicine, wrote that the clinical workforce in addiction treatment is "turning over at the same rate as that in the fast-food industry."[13] Your loved one might find himself working with a counselor who is very new to the field and has no prior experience with addictions. Too many facilities are staffed with caring people who know very little about the science of addiction treatment.

You, of course, also want a counselor who is knowledgeable about substance abuse *and* gay male issues. Unfortunately, such expertise is not the norm. Some counselors have no experience working with gay men, and others have limited exposure to substance abuse in their work. If you and your loved one are naïve about substance abuse treatment, you may obediently and blindly follow the protocol set by a practitioner. Too often the only recovery-specific recommendation a counselor offers is to find a Twelve Step meeting and start attending immediately. Other counselors jump right into sexuality issues, assuming that deeper concerns need to be explored before tackling drug use.

Counselors may work for agencies or independently. If you are considering using a counselor from an agency, I encourage you to use the list of agency guidelines in chapter 6 (pages 82–84) to explore his or her experience and skill in working with gay men and indeed all sexual minorities. Agency counselors often offer a more comprehensive approach because they are associated with a psychiatrist and medical doctor who can handle the possible myriad complications and co-occurring conditions associated with substance use.

## SUPPORTING MOTIVATION TO REMAIN IN TREATMENT

My office is located next to the pay phone at the treatment center where I work, and several times each week I overhear men in treatment call family members with one or more reasons why they simply can't stay in treatment. Often these reasons are so trivial and outright ludicrous that I begin to laugh behind my closed door: "I found a bug on the floor." "The food here is awful." "The other patients don't have the same problems I do." "I'm sick, and the doctor refuses to help me." This last one came from a man who saw the medical doctor four times in two days demanding addictive benzodiazepine medication for his anxiety, but who refused to experiment with safer options.

The early days to weeks of abstinence are *often* uncomfortable. Symptoms include body aches, fatigue, nausea, apathy, sleep problems, nervousness, and general irritability. The extent and duration of these symptoms depends on which substances were abused and for how long. Some men will need a formal detox or other medical supervision to get through this period. While eventually symptoms do diminish, some sooner than later, there is no doubt that early in a recovery effort, a man will experience discomfort, cravings, and possibly withdrawal symptoms. It is no wonder that so many people fail at recovery in the early days: they want to end their discomfort.

What can you do when your loved one's determination to stay abstinent for at least three months and to get help for his substance abuse begins to wane, or his resolve is fractured by physical symptoms? This is the time to

- Remind him why he is attempting abstinence and why he decided to get help in the first place.

- Be empathetic; he probably is experiencing discomfort.

- Encourage him to talk to those who are working with him on his recovery efforts, including treatment professionals, sponsors, and Twelve Step members. All may have valuable suggestions.

- Tell him you love him and you are proud of his effort.

If he does fail in his attempt, practice the tough-love approach described earlier. Put your needs first and take care of yourself. Remember you cannot rescue him from his mistake. When he sees your resolve not to rescue him, he'll likely try abstinence again pretty quickly. Over and over again, individuals in early recovery will try to convince themselves and the people who care for them that this is not the right time to stop using or to get help. They may come up with innumerable excuses. Be tough. Now is indeed the right time for your loved one to get help. If not now, when?

∷

Remember, the more active a family member or partner is in a loved one's treatment, the higher the odds of success. If your loved one does enter treatment—whether outpatient, inpatient, or a residential setting—stay involved. Ask for family sessions, attend family education meetings, and work to remain informed about his treatment. Confidentiality laws give your loved one the right to be selective in whom he will involve in his formal treatment and what can and cannot be disclosed to family members; for gay men, sex and sexuality concerns should usually be explored with a neutral professional before they are addressed with family. Doing so can help avoid uncomfortable situations for all. For example, one man offered an example of the power of methamphetamine on his life by revealing he had broken "three penis pumps in the last month while bingeing." His mother sat there confused, and his father blushed. This was more than they needed or wanted to hear.

Even if you are ready to charge right in and begin addressing these issues, he may not be ready. If you are his partner, you may feel comfortable addressing sexuality issues. But if you are a family member, you may be as reluctant as he is to talk about sex and sexuality issues, or even more so. Many family members who actively engage in treatment for substance use are stunningly distant and mute when it comes to the topic of sexual orientation. Without doubt, sex and sexuality issues will come to the forefront. If indeed you are uncomfortable with your loved one's sexual orientation and, even more worrisome, want to change it to heterosexual, you may ultimately hinder his recovery.

If you feel shame, guilt, and/or embarrassment over his sexuality, this will leak out even when you are sincerely trying to offer support. For both gay men and their family members who experience shame over sexual identity, the most pressing recurrent concern once initial stabilization has occurred is acceptance: acceptance of the immutability of his sexual orientation. Acceptance over the perceived losses that result from this. And, finally, acceptance that he can go on to create a satisfying and contented life that includes his sexual identity. Ideally, shame fades away and pride appears. If these latter goals seem hard to imagine, the information and stories in this book may help you see different possibilities. If you are indeed uncomfortable with your loved one's sexual orientation, your efforts on helping him through the initial stages of recovery will careen to an abrupt halt in the near future when you are challenged to actively engage with not just a substance-abusing man in treatment, but a substance-abusing *gay* man. If you really care about this man and want him to succeed in recovery, take some time to consider how you can offer complete and unwavering acceptance to him. Doing so will ultimately benefit him—and you—in untold ways.

## CHAPTER FIVE

# GETTING HELP— THE FIRST WEEKS

SOME GAY MEN REPORT that their orientation has nothing to do with their substance use; they believe that even if they were straight, they still would have developed a similar problem. For the majority though, the connection is thought to be either direct ("If I weren't gay, I wouldn't be an alcoholic") or at least one factor in their problem with drugs ("I drink because I'm lonely, and if I weren't a gay man, I wouldn't be so lonely"). Many gay men enter treatment eager to work on issues related to their orientation, incorrectly believing that this alone will resolve their substance use problems. In reality, sexual orientation is but one of many issues that need to be examined early in treatment.

Abstinence is always the starting point for dealing with substance abuse issues, even if the abuser is determined to drink or use drugs again in the future. Some men will not consider abstinence, even temporarily; chapter 9 explores the possibilities and pitfalls of controlled moderate drug use. Abstinence is necessary for anyone seeking help for substance use, regardless of orientation, but the recommendations and suggestions for achieving abstinence are somewhat different for gay men. They cannot simply follow the exact same protocol that has been so successful for straight men and women due to a series of recognized challenges:

- The vast majority of research on addictions treatment has been with straight men; we are still learning about the special needs of gay men in recovery. Most current treatment approaches fail to recognize or understand the importance of gay male issues.

- Most people seeking help for substance use problems turn to a Twelve Step approach. Twelve Steppers are proud to inform you that no matter where you are in the United States, you can easily find a meeting. While this may be a bit of an overstatement, locating a meeting is relatively uncomplicated for people who are straight. Meetings that feel safe for gay men, and sincerely welcome them, are more difficult to find.

- The Twelve Step approach promotes acceptance of a Higher Power. Yet, understandably, many gay men resent this spiritual approach because they do not find acceptance in so many organized religions.

- Many people need inpatient treatment (such as detox and/or rehab). Many of these settings are not accepting of GLBT people.

- Both outpatient and couples counseling are important components of addictions treatment. We not only want a therapist who has the best interests of our loved one at heart but one who also has a knowledge base regarding substance abuse and addiction. The downside to using a therapist who is a "generalist" is that he or she may not have a comprehensive understanding of addiction and recovery. Finally, we need a therapist familiar with gay men and their most common issues. Trying to locate a therapist who meets all of these requirements—trustworthy, knowledgeable about gay male issues, and competent to treat substance abuse concerns—often becomes a difficult quest.

- Gay men have very few social and recreational settings to go to that do not involve some type of substance use. In comparison to straight men and women, they have far fewer places where they can socialize without the presence of one or more addictive substances.

- Far more than with any other demographic group, gay male substance use issues overlap with sexual activity. Too many gay men may have no experience of satisfying sex that does not involve drug use.

- Because substance use is so prevalent in the gay male community, our views of what is normal have been skewed. With so many gay men using one or more addictive substances, even if recreationally, it is far more difficult to recognize when one man is having a problem with drugs or alcohol.

Keeping the above challenges in mind, this chapter addresses the most pressing concerns gay men have during their first few weeks of abstinence, wherever that abstinence takes place (detox, home, inpatient or outpatient setting, or any combination of these options).

## WITHDRAWAL

For a person without a substance use problem, stopping use for several months sounds easy. But for many men, their history of drug use makes simply stopping a substantial undertaking. Let's consider some of the early challenges they may face.

Withdrawal symptoms are common, ranging from the mildly discomforting to the torturous. Even regular coffee drinkers go through withdrawal after a day or so without caffeine—unpleasant, but certainly not insurmountable. The choice of substances and the length of time abused affect the severity of the withdrawal symptoms. Also, many people have little tolerance for painful and/or unpleasant sensations. This may have been one of the reasons that they found drug use so appealing in the first place: It blocked or masked emotional and physical pain and discomfort that is simply part of their physiological makeup. Thus the discomfort that comes with ending drug use is simply too much for these sensitive people to bear. They have probably tried to quit before and memories of these unpleasant withdrawal symptoms prevent them from making another attempt to stop.

Withdrawal from some drugs—particularly central nervous system depressants such as Xanax, Ativan, Valium, and alcohol—can endanger one's health, and men addicted to these drugs often need medical supervision when they quit using. Withdrawal from these drugs can lead to seizures and even death.

Withdrawal from stimulants (such as meth and cocaine) usually requires days of sleep. By the time they are trying to end their drug use, these men have typically been on a long series of binges and are physically exhausted. Once the physical exhaustion lifts, cravings often reappear.

Inpatient treatment with its supportive staff and lack of triggers may be the only setting that can prevent a man from answering the siren call of his cravings.

Withdrawal from opioids (heroin, Vicodin, Percodan, Oxycontin, and Demerol, to name a few), though rarely dangerous, is often agonizing. This class of drugs tends to have the most unsettling and uncomfortable withdrawal symptoms. A person withdrawing from alcohol may look awful as his body trembles uncontrollably from delirium tremens, shaking so badly that he can't even write his name, yet he'll tell you he is feeling more or less okay. In contrast, people in early recovery from an opioid addiction tend to look fairly stable externally but will often be feeling extreme (and sometimes unbearable) discomfort. In the early stages of abstinence, the physical withdrawal symptoms from this class of drugs are unrelenting. Many men are unable to tolerate them and so return to drugs use to end the physical torment. It's typical for those going through opioid withdrawal to have a medically managed detox.

Withdrawing from other drugs such as marijuana and hallucinogens (including Ecstasy) does not typically cause adverse symptoms. They may be uncomfortable, but are more of an annoyance than painful.

## Detox

Most gay men will try to quit drugs on their own without formal treatment; many use just a self-help and/or Twelve Step approach. While some find success this way, others need more formal treatment, such as outpatient and inpatient treatment, rehab, and detoxification.

If you know that he has a low tolerance for discomfort, that a past quit attempt was excruciating, and/or that he is using a drug that is usually more difficult or dangerous to withdraw from, suggest that he ask for help from a medical provider, or help him explore the benefits of a detoxification program. Medicine has numerous interventions to reduce the discomfort of ending substance use. With medical help, some people sail through their first week of clean time effortlessly. Others may still feel some discomfort, but it will be far more tolerable, and the chances of staying drug free through the first few days will be exponentially more likely. Medically supervised detox is now a fairly painless experience, and within days most symptoms are gone.

Detoxification can take place in an inpatient or outpatient setting. In an inpatient setting, a person will receive medication to help with physical symptoms, lots of bed rest, vitamins, a quality diet, treatment for any co-occurring medical problems (such as diabetes, depression, heart disease, or any other medical issue), and basic drug abuse education. At the end of his inpatient stay, he'll be referred to some form of outpatient treatment as follow-up. Fortunately, most people can detox on an outpatient basis.

The advantage of an outpatient detox is that there is less change to one's daily life; he is able to remain at home; and some people find that they can work during this time period. However, if home is filled with triggers that will initiate a return to drug use, a brief respite from this environment may be just what he needs. During this time away, a partner or friends can rid the house of any items connected with drug use (such as emptying the liquor cupboard or destroying drug paraphernalia). He might also benefit from the inpatient route if he has psychiatric and/or health problems that may complicate the first few days of abstinence.

## REHAB

Many people leaving detox are referred to an inpatient rehabilitation setting. But any person experiencing a drug use problem can *try* to enter a rehab; it is not strictly for people leaving a detox. Notice the stress on the word "try"; gaining entrance to a rehab facility is increasingly difficult under managed care. Inpatient rehab settings offer twenty-four-hour observation, monitoring, and treatment. Emergency medical services, individual and group counseling, psychiatric evaluation and treatment, and family involvement are all typical services offered in inpatient rehab. Until fairly recently the standard length of stay in rehab was twenty-eight days, but as research finds that much of what is accomplished in this setting can occur in a (far less expensive) outpatient setting, the length of stay has decreased, often markedly.

The American Society of Addiction Medicine (ASAM) developed a set of criteria for the placement of drug and alcohol abusers in treatment settings. If the abuser is paying out of pocket and can afford the fees of an inpatient rehab facility, you can be sure that it will open its doors to him. If, on the other hand, he is using insurance to help pay for treatment, then reviewers will use the ASAM criteria to determine the appropriate level of care for his situation. Just wanting inpatient treatment no longer guarantees he will receive it. With prices at some high-end facilities exceeding one thousand dollars per day, treatment choices are based as much on financial considerations as on drug use history. What does insurance cover? It is not uncommon for an insurer to cover a week or less of rehab treatment. Thus, he may have to negotiate with his insurance company to maximize his benefits.

Here are some of the factors insurance companies look at when determining the need for inpatient substance abuse treatment:

- Has he had untreated or symptomatic co-occurring psychiatric conditions (including mental health issues such as depression, schizophrenia, or bipolar disorder, to name just a few)?

- Is he at risk for suicide or other self-harm (such as cutting or purging) behaviors?

- Has he behaved in ways that may put others at risk for harm?

- Does he have any underlying medical problems that complicate recovery?

- Has he failed at past recovery efforts (including unsuccessful outpatient treatment)?

- Is he employed in a position in which continued substance use could endanger the public (for example, a medical professional, bus driver, or pilot)?

- Does his living environment present numerous risks for relapse (such as living with other substance users; risk of victimization to the substance user if he returns home)?

In summary, an inpatient rehab setting is for the person who cannot succeed in the early weeks of treatment without intensive round-the-clock monitoring and support. Most substance abusers will not need a rehab; even those leaving a detox setting often forgo this treatment model. Still, if you believe that his current living environment poses a threat to abstinence, examine the availability of an inpatient rehab facility.

In addition to detox and rehab, there are other options to consider in the early weeks of recovery. There are halfway house programs (structured residential programs lasting three months), long-term residential programs, and even boot camp settings. Unfortunately, private insurance rarely covers these programs, and he will need to pay out of pocket.

## Inpatient Treatment Considerations

For those who need inpatient treatment, even if only in these very early days of recovery, there are pros and cons. One pro is that residential facilities minimize risks of relapse because the substance abuse cues that abound in one's home environment are missing. And even if one is strongly tempted to use or experiences overpowering cravings, there is always a staff member or peer on hand to quell these emotions. One con is that inpatient settings do not offer an oasis of peace; some of his peers in these programs will have serious mental health problems. Indeed, living with such individuals in these settings is often a task in itself. Believe me when I tell you that he will find at least one peer and one staff member who will aggravate him to no end.

Finally, and of major importance to readers of this book, unless he is entering a gay-specific facility, he may encounter heterosexism and homo-hatred. This is one potential big con.

After months of repeatedly seeing the same magazine titles available at the admissions area of a large behavioral health hospital, a gay male staff member unobtrusively inserted a trendy gay-themed magazine into the pile. The periodical was definitely tailored for the fashion-conscious gay man, but was no more overtly sexual than the female-oriented magazines that were offered. Still, when a housekeeping staffer found it, she took it to the head of the admissions department, who proceeded to toss it into the trash, muttering that some patients "might be insulted." *Is this a significant indicator of the facility's approach to gay men? Would you want a gay man to obtain treatment there?*

I sometimes monitor counseling and therapy groups and am shocked to hear the gay-baiting and outright hostility toward gay men. Yet few people challenge these sentiments, including staff. All it takes is one person to politely say that such language makes treatment unsafe and is therefore unwelcome. Personalized comments from staff or other community members (such as, "I have an uncle who is gay, and I disagree with what you're saying") can shut down even the most strident bigot. If this doesn't happen, he can ask for a meeting with the supervisor and complain or talk with a trusted counselor to initiate change. If there is any indication that negativity toward gay men is rampant in the facility, get him the hell out of there. Make sure he is using the services of a facility that respects him.

In *A Provider's Introduction to Substance Abuse Treatment for Lesbian, Gay, Bisexual, and Transgender Individuals,* the Center for Substance Abuse Treatment lists specific ways that substance abuse treatment providers can demonstrate that they are experienced in working with sexual minorities. In my experience, I find that the questions below are

## QUESTIONS TO ASK INPATIENT TREATMENT PROVIDERS

- Is *all* staff required to participate in trainings relating to sexual minorities?

- Do the forms, brochures, and educational materials *assume* heterosexuality as the norm?

- Does the facility promote and advertise its GLBT services?

- Does the facility's referral and resource list offer options relevant to gay men?

- Are there GLBT Twelve Step meetings available during treatment? If not, is it safe for a gay man to share in existing meetings?

- Does the facility make family services available for domestic partners and other loved ones involved in a gay man's treatment?

- Do education sessions and lectures include GLBT issues?

- Does the facility employ openly gay individuals as staff members?

- What are the guidelines for clients regarding homophobic behavior so that GLBT individuals are safe? How are these guidelines enforced?

- Does the facility provide education for heterosexual clients about language and behaviors that show bias toward GLBT people?

- How does the facility investigate complaints of discriminatory practices reported by GLBT clients and family members?

most telling about a treatment facility. I encourage you, your loved one, or any concerned others to ask these questions when looking for a treatment provider.[1]

If we all start asking these questions, facilities will eventually respond by improving their services for gay men. If you are involved in helping find a treatment facility for a client or loved one, please ask these questions before you choose one particular treatment center.

Keep in mind that inpatient treatment facilities such as detox and rehab are short-term and not geared to resolve long-term issues. As Candy Finnigan, an addiction specialist on the television series *Intervention*, says, residential treatment centers "create a period of sobriety or abstinence—from substances or behaviors—that provide time and security for everybody concerned, nothing more. They provide a new environment that furnishes healthy routines, backed by consistent feedback and discipline. That's a big deal, and it's important for a good start on your new life. But much more is called for. . . ."[2]

Don't expect most facilities to excel in working with gay men or to consider sexual identity issues important to address during treatment. If you find a facility that is respectful of gay men and their families (particularly their romantic partners), and does its best to weed out heterosexist assumptions and behaviors, you have probably found a safe place. Finding such a facility is not easy; even high-end luxury programs are guilty of heterosexism and homophobia.

## MEDICATIONS

There are medications available to help in the early days of abstinence. Some are used in the detox process to lessen withdrawal symptoms. Others help reduce cravings and urges to return to substance use. Some reduce the euphoria a person feels from drug use, thus short-circuiting their reward. The following is a list of medications most commonly seen in the early recovery stage that may be used for a period ranging from weeks to months.

- Antabuse (disulfiram)—The first medication to receive FDA approval for alcohol dependency. A person who drinks while on this medication becomes violently ill.

- ReVia and Vivitrol (naltrexone)—This medication blocks the euphoria of alcohol use and reduces craving for the substance. Naltrexone comes in two forms. ReVia is a pill form taken daily, and Vivitrol is an injectable form given every twenty-eight days.

- Campral (acamprosate calcium)—A medication that reduces cravings for alcohol. It has been used in Europe for over a decade but was only recently introduced in the United States.

- Methadone—A medication that reduces cravings and blocks the rewarding aspects of opioid use. It is most often used for heroin addiction and is a controversial drug even after decades of successful outcomes because users become physically dependent on the medication.

- Suboxone (buprenorphine)—This medication also reduces cravings and blocks the reward of opioid use. It is now increasingly used for narcotic painkiller addiction and can be prescribed by a doctor rather than obtained through daily clinic visits as required for methadone.

Other medications are slowly working their way down the admittedly sparse pipeline, and the one currently garnering the most attention is a vaccine for cocaine abuse. In all cases, medication by itself will not solve a substance use problem; recovery is an active process that requires changes in thinking, behaviors, and lifestyle.

## POST-ACUTE WITHDRAWAL SYMPTOMS

While withdrawal symptoms quickly resolve, some drugs lead to changes in mood, emotions, and memory that take far longer to clear up. These can continue on for weeks, and in some cases months. Cocaine withdrawal, for example, can lead to anxiety, depression, and insomnia for weeks after its last use. Similar symptoms from methamphetamine use typically last for months. Other common complaints include problems with short-term memory. The inability to experience pleasure is another complaint many people have in early treatment.

Although these symptoms are definitely uncomfortable, they will resolve over time. Returning to substance use may offer temporary relief
but will not improve them in the long-term. Instead, they will get worse.

:::

The first few days to weeks of abstinence are the most physically uncomfortable and (depending on one's health history and drug choice) dangerous. Still, there are ways to get through these days safely and with a
minimum of discomfort. Again, this is not always a lifelong commitment;
some men may be able to return to controlled drug use. For others, even a
one-time experiment risks a return to all of the negative repercussions of
addiction they so valiantly sought to escape. For now though, he needs to
focus on getting through several months of early recovery without revert-
ing to any substance use.

## CHAPTER SIX

# GETTING HELP—
# THE COUNSELOR'S ROLE

COUNSELORS CAN PLAY an important role in helping newly recovering gay men be successful in their early recovery, and in maintaining long-term recovery. There are many pitfalls these men can avoid with the guidance of a skilled counselor.

I recommend that gay men work with counselors who have gay affirmative practices—counselors who show respect for the gay male lifestyle and culture and acknowledge the personal integrity of a gay man's sexuality. If you offer treatment to gay men, the recommendations of the American Psychological Association (APA), though targeting psychologists in particular, are instructive for all helping professionals.

## THE GOALS OF COUNSELING IN EARLY RECOVERY

The overarching goals of counseling in early recovery are abstinence and psychiatric and health stabilization. Other goals, though very important, must take a secondary role. Ken, for example, even though abstinent only eight days, wanted to work on healing his inner child. Curt requested psychological help for coming out to his family—he had been drug free less than a week. Wayne's shame about his childhood sexual victimization haunted him; now one month abstinent, he felt that he wanted to confront his inner demons. In all three cases, I offered the same recommendation: It is too early to focus on these issues. They may be profoundly

# APA Guidelines for Psychotherapy with Lesbian, Gay, and Bisexual Clients

## ATTITUDES TOWARD HOMOSEXUALITY AND BISEXUALITY

- **Guideline 1.** Psychologists understand that homosexuality and bisexuality are not indicative of mental illness.

- **Guideline 2.** Psychologists are encouraged to recognize how their attitudes and knowledge about lesbian, gay, and bisexual issues may be relevant to assessment and treatment and seek consultation or make appropriate referrals when indicated.

- **Guideline 3.** Psychologists strive to understand the ways in which social stigmatization (i.e., prejudice, discrimination, and violence) poses risks to the mental health and well-being of lesbian, gay, and bisexual clients.

- **Guideline 4.** Psychologists strive to understand how inaccurate or prejudicial views of homosexuality or bisexuality may affect the client's presentation in treatment and the therapeutic process.

## RELATIONSHIPS AND FAMILIES

- **Guideline 5.** Psychologists strive to be knowledgeable about and respect the importance of lesbian, gay, and bisexual relationships.

- **Guideline 6.** Psychologists strive to understand the particular circumstances and challenges facing lesbian, gay, and bisexual parents.

- **Guideline 7.** Psychologists recognize that the families of lesbian, gay, and bisexual people may include people who are not legally or biologically related.

- **Guideline 8.** Psychologists strive to understand how a person's homosexual or bisexual orientation may have an impact on his or her family of origin and the relationship to that family of origin.

*continues*

## ISSUES OF DIVERSITY

- **Guideline 9.** Psychologists are encouraged to recognize the particular life issues or challenges experienced by lesbian, gay, and bisexual members of racial and ethnic minorities that are related to multiple and often conflicting cultural norms, values, and beliefs.

- **Guideline 10.** Psychologists are encouraged to recognize the particular challenges experienced by bisexual individuals.

- **Guideline 11.** Psychologists strive to understand the special problems and risks that exist for lesbian, gay, and bisexual youth.

- **Guideline 12.** Psychologists consider generational differences within lesbian, gay, and bisexual populations, and the particular challenges that may be experienced by lesbian, gay, and bisexual older adults.

- **Guideline 13.** Psychologists are encouraged to recognize the particular challenges experienced by lesbian, gay, and bisexual individuals with physical, sensory, and/or cognitive/emotional disabilities.

## EDUCATION

- **Guideline 14.** Psychologists support the provision of professional education and training on lesbian, gay, and bisexual issues.

- **Guideline 15.** Psychologists are encouraged to increase their knowledge and understanding of homosexuality and bisexuality through continuing education, training, supervision, and consultation.

- **Guideline 16.** Psychologists make reasonable efforts to familiarize themselves with relevant mental health, educational, and community resources for lesbian, gay, and bisexual people.[1]

When working with substance-abusing sexual minorities in particular, the Substance Abuse and Mental Health Services Administration of the U.S. Department of Health and Human Services recommends the following six critical guidelines:[2]

1. Helping professionals should self-monitor for their own biases regarding gay men.

continues

2. Helping professionals should continue to receive training on sexual minorities and the issues they present in treatment.

3. Helping professionals should assist their clients in healing from the negative effects of homophobia and heterosexism.

4. Helping professionals should help their clients regain their personal power, including improving their self-concept and self-confidence.

5. Helping professionals should create a safe and supportive environment in which gay men can share their concerns.

6. Helping professionals should acknowledge gay men's significant others and loved ones.

important and may truly need to be addressed to achieve a satisfying life, but the goal of the first several months of counseling is to become stable and abstinent. Early counseling examines risks and triggers for relapse and helps a recovering person pragmatically and logistically make changes in his lifestyle that support clean and sober living.

I meet many men who after a week of abstinence are already reimagining their lives. Their musings are as grounded as stating that they plan on growing wings to star as the celestial being in the Broadway revival of *Angels in America*. They remain insubstantial dreams until their substance use has been stopped or controlled; a return to substance use can put the kibosh on all one's dreams and aspirations.

## Co-occurring Drug Use

Many gay men are abusing more than one substance, and they may hold to a belief that they need to stop only one of them, typically the one they see as the most damaging. In their eyes, they are abusing or addicted to only one drug. They'll readily give up meth, for example, but continue to drink. Success with such a plan is very unlikely for two main reasons: First, using one drug is likely to trigger a craving for other substances. Second, quitting only one drug all too often leads to an increase in use of the other drug. Counselors can easily spot this kind of faulty thinking and steer the newly recovering person back on track. They understand that the more severe the substance use, the more likely it's about coping with a variety of problems, stressors, and dilemmas. Having any drug to fall back on prevents many opportunities for personal growth and development.

## Coexisting Addictions

Addiction once referred to the misuse of drugs and alcohol, but the more we learn about the condition (and its origins in the brain) the more similarities we see to other addictions that don't involve substance use. If a man has an addiction to one or more drugs, he is more likely to have other compulsive problems. The most common include sex, food, shopping, gambling, exercise, and work (that is, "workaholism").

Resolving a substance use issue does not mean that a coexisting addiction is similarly resolved. Instead these coexisting addictions can become worse as substance use decreases or ends. Additional addictions can also complicate a recovery plan, making it more unlikely that he will be successful in ending or decreasing his substance use. Again, the support of a counselor to help him untangle and address coexisting addictions can be invaluable.

## Co-occurring Disorders

About 50 percent of people with substance abuse problems also struggle with a psychological problem—which has existed even before they began using substances. Common psychological problems encountered in substance abuse treatment include

- bipolar disorder

- depression

- anxiety

- trauma

- schizophrenia

- attention deficit disorder

Many men may have started drug use as a form of self-medication—to deal with the dismaying symptoms of one of these common psychological disorders. And while many of these conditions are successfully treated with medications, the compliance rate is less than heartening. People simply stop taking medications due to inconvenience, side effects, or stubbornness. Soon afterward symptoms return and abstinence falls to the wayside. For this reason, maintaining psychiatric stability is essential to successful abstinence.

In addition, underlying medical problems can complicate abstinence efforts. These health problems—such as heart and kidney problems, diabetes, infectious diseases, liver damage, substance use–related accidents and injuries, changes in sleep patterns, weight changes, hypertension, and gastrointestinal problems—may have existed before substance use occurred, may have developed alongside drug use, or may be the result of the drug use. It's critical, then, that medical problems be addressed by appropriate medical personnel and stabilized.

## Sexuality Issues

Should sexuality issues be addressed for gay men in early recovery? Here's what Joe Amico, President of the National Association of Lesbian and Gay Addiction Professionals, has to say on the subject:

> I believe it is extremely important to address sexuality issues in early treatment. Several researchers and documents have pointed out that confusion and/or shame around sexual identity and/or sexual orientation issues contribute to substance abuse. What that translates for me is that the most potential for relapse comes during these early stages of coming out, so if we don't address those issues in treatment, how can we expect those individuals to stay sober? Those treatment programs that continue to say things like "deal with your sobriety first and your sexuality later" are contributing to relapse potential in the same way that programs used to say "deal with sobriety first and then your mental health issues." We now know that best practices require co-occurring treatment rather than the sobriety now and mental health later.[3]

Amico's experience is that two-thirds of gay men entering treatment for substance abuse issues are in the very early stages of coming out; they can't even accept their own sexuality and may even find it undesirable. In the early weeks of counseling such men, the best approach is an affirmative one. When counselors and other helping professionals approach gay men by affirming their sexual orientation and by examining how heterosexism affects their lives, they are on the right road. Any hint of suggestion that their sexual orientation is pathological, or shameful, can thwart attempts to bolster their self-esteem and their confidence that they can deal with tough feelings without using and abusing alcohol and other drugs.

Counselors can do a great service by helping gay male clients verbalize their shame and internalized homophobia (also called internalized heterosexism) and by working to create a safe relationship in which these men, and any helping professionals, fully accept their sexuality. Depending on what stage of coming out he is in, counselors may not even ask the client to describe himself as "gay." Many gay men cannot accept this identity early on in treatment; even the label can cause them panic. Leaving their sexual identity open for exploration might indeed be the best intervention. Direct confrontation of men who are unsure about their sexual identity is inadvisable.

As his life becomes even more stable, he will be more capable of exploring the numerous issues affected by his sexuality. But in these early days of counseling, safety and acceptance are the priorities.

## Talking about Sexual Activity in Counseling

Due to their own discomfort and shame, counselors who are not skilled at counseling gay clients rarely touch on the topic of sex, particularly gay sex. In such cases, it is important to make sure that the topic of sex and drug use during sexual activity is being addressed in counseling; gay men in particular seem to be challenged by the connection between sex and substance use. Whether it is anonymous sex, prostitution, pornography, or online communications, drug use plays a recurrent role:

- Some drugs increase sexual desire and appetite; methamphetamine is the most notable example.

- Some drugs directly affect sexual performance. For example, cocaine can cause delayed ejaculation. Poppers cause vasodilation and make anal sex easier and more pleasurable. Methamphetamine decreases refraction time—the time required before a man can experience sexual arousal again after ejaculation.

• Drug use lowers inhibitions. This is particularly true for gay men
  who feel shame. If they believe that gay sexual activity is wrong and
  sinful, drug use can temporarily conceal these emotions, or at least
  until ejaculation. Drugs also cloud one's awareness, desire, and even
  intention to protect oneself from dangerous practices. Recognizing
  that a potential sex partner may carry HIV or some other disease
  can certainly put a damper on one's sexual desires. But after a few
  drinks or use of other drugs, this awareness is conveniently forgotten, at least until the panic sets in when the drug wears off.

Counselors won't ask a client to be celibate (unless he has a co-
occurring sexual addiction; a period of mandatory celibacy is then a standard treatment goal), but in the client's effort to avoid people, places, and
things associated with drug cravings, this naturally includes high-risk
sexual scenarios. For now, he must abstain from any type of sexual activity associated with substance use.

## THE COMING-OUT PROCESS

Coming out as a gay man is a process, not a singular event. If he does it
at all, he will likely have to disclose his identity many, many times in his
life. The very first few times may be terrifying, particularly when it comes
time to broach the topic with parents and siblings, but from that point on,
each time he meets a new potential friend, a new colleague, a new church
member, starts a new job, and moves to a new home, he will have to make
an often-uncomfortable decision for or against disclosure. Even the most
out gay man repeatedly finds himself in situations where he must disclose
his sexuality; otherwise people who are unfamiliar with him presume he
is straight due to heterosexuality as the assumed status quo.

Many (if not most) treatment facilities assume that a new client is
straight unless told otherwise. Some gay men are completely up front
about their sexuality with everyone they meet, even passing strangers; others take their secret to their grave. Your client or loved one will
fit somewhere along this continuum. The matrix of decision making
depends on his comfort with his identity, his experiences with disclosure, and the current environment in which he finds himself. Many gay
men, for example, are out to families and friends but not at all in their

workplaces. And, of course, not coming out as a gay man and even passing as straight are probably the wisest decisions he can make in certain
situations. But if he is unyielding in this stance, adopting it as a generalized pretense in all situations, we have reason to be wary.

Given societal barriers and lack of support, consider the astounding
amount of work it must take for a gay man to evolve from a teen confused and embarrassed about his sexuality to an adult who embraces his
identity with pride. Don't assume that due to the number of "out" lumi-
naries, gay characters in the media, and increasing acceptance of sexual minorities that gay youth and adults no longer struggle with their
identity. They still do, and they can become trapped at an earlier stage
of identity development. There are several competing theories on sexual
identity formation; the resources section at the end of the book includes
suggested readings and web sites on this topic.

The Cass Model is the most well known and empirically supported,
and it hypothesizes that sexual minorities move through six stages of
development, the final two being pride and integration of sexual orientation into one's identity.[4] This process of identity formation can be stifled
or outright derailed at any of these stages. In the beginning a gay man
recognizes that he has same-sex desires, but these are minimized and/or
ignored. As these desires become more evident and unavoidable, he must
either accept them, rail against them, or exert much energy to deny them
to himself and others. Men who use the latter two tactics often begin using drugs to cope with the internal conflict that this desire causes in their
lives, making further growth impossible. Many gay men stop their development at these early stages, and some professionals (myself included)
believe that these men cannot move forward again until they have a sizable amount of clean time—often more than a year. Dana Finnegan and
Emily McNally describe this well in their book *Counseling Lesbian, Gay,
Bisexual, and Transgender Substance Abusers*:

> There are, of course, numerous strategies for foreclosure. . . . Using alco-
> hol and drugs is a major one and if the use becomes problematic, then
> the denial in response to homophobia is joined by the denial of alcohol
> and drug problems. Other foreclosure tactics may be a refusal to "hear"
> any more information about the subject; inhibit sexual desire (become
> asexual); marry; pursue a course of hypersexual heterosexuality; pray;
> seek a "cure"; rationalize and redefine the feelings and behavior ("We're

just friends": "I was drunk and didn't know what I was doing"). . . .
People have an enormously high investment in being okay in their own
and the world's eyes. Their psychic survival depends, therefore, on denial and any other defense that will help them block off the terrifying
knowledge of who they are or might be.[5]

The point at which substance use becomes problematic is also when
emotional maturity stops and general maturation come to a standstill.
The same holds true for sexual identity formation. The young teen bewil-
dered and frightened over his blossoming sexual identity inadvertently
discovers the wonders of pharmaceuticals freely available in his parents'
medicine cabinet. While this serves as a balm for his inner turmoil, it also
forestalls the struggles he must undergo in the crucible of identity formation. He could well end up a married man in his thirties who has numerous hidden sexual flings with men, all the while hoping to disown this
secret part of himself (in addition to having learned to use substances—
both licit and illicit—to cope with emotional discomfort).

Don't assume that those young gay men who crowd the dance floors
of the local club are anywhere near to crystallizing their identity formation. In my work, the most tragic encounters I have with gay men, even
those men who seem to have it all, is their desire to be straight and to
blame their sexual identity for all of the problems in their lives. Most often it is these same men who lean on drugs and alcohol to soothe their
shame (particularly if they are leading a double life), to bolster their identity, and to allow themselves to engage in sexual contact with another
man. Only by ending reliance on drug use can these men advance to a
higher level of identity development, one in which they find joy, satisfaction, and pleasure in their lives and identities as gay men.


## PEOPLE, PLACES, AND THINGS

"Avoiding people, places, and things" may be the most overworked
phrase in the world of recovery. Its relevance goes without saying, but
still many people do not incorporate this simple principle into their lives
early in recovery. If an addict associates certain individuals, events, loca-
tions, and/or objects with substance use, their presence will be not only
reminders of drug use but also temptations. Regular visits to a counselor

can help newly recovering gay men identify their triggers, and figure out how to avoid them, or replace those people, places, and things with new people, places, and things. Still, this is not an easy task.

Kyle, for example, is an alcoholic whose pattern was to start drinking on Friday night at his favorite bar with friends and then continue on through Sunday night alone in his apartment. Returning to that same bar is just too much of a risk in Kyle's early days of abstinence. Even spending time with the same friends could jeopardize his efforts to stay dry. Maybe in the future he will be able to return to that same bar without succumbing to the urge to drink. Maybe in the future he'll be able to socialize with his friends while they imbibe and yet remain abstinent himself. However, these scenarios are in the future; they may or may not occur. What is certain is that if Kyle goes to this "place" or hangs out with these "people," he will likely start drinking again.

In the first few months of abstinence, gay men face the same stressors and unpleasant emotions that everyone encounters in life, regardless of substance use. But now, these will be temptations for him to begin drinking or using again. Why add fuel to the fire by choosing to be around relapse-potentiating "people, places, and things"?

## Coping with Cravings

Encountering a "person, place, or thing" formerly linked with substance use can lead to physical longings for drug use and/or the inability to rid the mind of thoughts of such use. Cravings can arise suddenly and overwhelm one's coping ability; a typical outcome in such scenarios is, of course, a return to substance use. Obviously, the best way to dodge cravings is to avoid people, places, and things once associated with substance use. But despite one's best efforts, reminders of drug use can slip past these defenses. Weslen, for example, was four months clean and quite proud of his accomplishment. One night at a restaurant he ran into a group of former drinking cronies that he had politely managed to avoid since he had become sober. They invited him to join them at the bar after dinner, where he was soon deluged and nearly overcome with an almost visceral desire for "just one drink."

However, cravings do not arise only when one is confronted with external reminders of substance use. Emotions can also rouse cravings. If a man drinks to cope with anger or shame, these emotions themselves become associated with alcohol use. When he experiences these emotions again during a period of abstinence, his brain naturally sets in motion a desire for the same source of succor—in this case alcohol—that quelled this emotion in the past. Indeed, anytime a person is experiencing a lack of pleasure in life, cravings are a reminder from the brain that there is a quick way to improve one's mood or alleviate distress. Finally, cravings can also stem from positive scenarios and emotions. Many men have a history of using various substances to further enhance positive experiences. For example, someone may use alcohol to make social interactions more enjoyable and spontaneous, and sexual arousal is a common craving trigger for gay men, since they often use drugs to intensify sexual activity.

Counselors will help recovering addicts find ways to recognize and short-circuit cravings before they spiral into substance use. Most cravings

---

### HOW TO SHORT-CIRCUIT CRAVINGS

- *Distract yourself.* Keep a list of safe activities you can engage in when cravings arise. Peter, for example, found that craving periods were the ideal time to do his laundry. Many gay men may opt instead to hit the gym.

- *Talk with others.* If you have a sponsor in your Twelve Step program, this is the ideal time to pick up the phone and call him or her. (Partners—don't be hurt if your loved one doesn't reveal his cravings to you, at least not in the beginning. What is important is that he talks about them with a safe person.)

- *Recall the negative consequences of using drugs.* Some men carry a list of the damage they did while abusing substances, as well as a list of the benefits of abstinence.

- *Remember that cravings and urges are normal.* They are not a sign of failure and do not have to lead to substance use. The objective is to learn your triggers and cues for cravings and then avoid or eliminate them.

- *Remember that cravings lessen over time.* Cravings will only get stronger to a point; they then start to go away.

- *Remember that cravings grow stronger if you give in to them.*

will fade away in less than an hour. There are a wide variety of strategies for coping with cravings. The list "How to Short-Circuit Cravings" on the previous page describes some successful methods. If you are a counselor, you may already use some of the same tools to help clients deal with their feelings of sadness, shame, and fear without picking up a drug or a drink.

## Expanding a Repertoire

When substance abusers are actively using, most tend to pull away from non-drug-related activities and friends. This starts off slowly and builds until the substance abuser is eventually surrounded by a peer group, social settings, pastimes, and activities that all support continued use. Once positive (or at least neutral) people, places, and things are replaced by those supportive of drug use. Those not supportive of this new lifestyle are removed from your loved one's life or at least pushed to the sidelines. What happens, then, when he attempts to reclaim his old interests or even try out new activities?

Drug use exaggerates the feel-good chemical dopamine in the brain to a far greater extent than any other "natural" reinforcer, including food and sex. Joseph, for example was a confirmed theatergoer, at least until his meth use surpassed his desire for Broadway outings (and his ability to finance such jaunts). Now two months into recovery, he took a trip to New York City for three days of musicals, including two evening shows and a matinee. He expressed his disappointment upon his return; Broadway just didn't have the same allure and "bang" that it had before. This makes sense, for how could any show—no matter how elaborate the spectacle—compare to the brain stimulation of meth? The best advice is to give it time; your loved one can relearn to enjoy those former pastimes that once offered pleasure in his life, and he can also venture out and explore new adventures and opportunities. Eventually his brain will readjust to the less extreme highs and lows of drug-free living.

## Free Time

Learning to use free time productively also helps when working to expand one's repertoire. Many people in recovery from substance use problems have too much free time. They once filled their waking hours with obtaining, using, and recovering from their drug use. When these activities are no longer a part of their lives, many are left with a void, especially in the early days of recovery. They have nothing that satisfactorily fills their time. This problem is about more than being bored; it's further complicated because the brain-based dopamine rush of substance use far surpasses the enjoyment that pre–substance use activities produced.

Empty time not only swamps a newly recovering person with boredom (an emotion abhorred by many in early recovery) but also offers that person ample opportunity to think about their using days. Some of this reverie may include happy memories of substance use or, conversely, self-flagellation over how much one has destroyed one's life (along with accompanying shame and guilt). Obviously, neither recollection supports abstinence. Finally, the more one's life was ruled by substance use, the more chaotic it became. It is not surprising that many newly recovering men no longer have any set schedule—their using days were lived in an impulsive and disorganized manner. Indeed, one of the goals of rehab is to reintroduce patients to a set schedule, including set meals, bedtimes, and group schedules. A chaotic lifestyle breeds relapse.

Structuring one's days and avoiding too much free time is important, at least for the first several weeks. Your loved one will likely be given a daily schedule so he can plan out each day. He will be encouraged to fill his time with meetings, counseling, visiting with sober friends, exercise, and other activities that support abstinence and to not leave more than two hours of unscheduled time other than that devoted to sleeping.

## EMOTIONS

Learning to deal with difficult feelings is another very important task to work on in recovery. Drug use can relieve (at least temporarily) uncomfortable emotions. Many people struggle with negative emotions, and this is particularly true for those with substance abuse problems. Consider the following list of feelings that, if handled poorly, can threaten recovery:

- frustration

- resentment

- anger

- shame

- guilt

- loneliness

- boredom

It is part of human nature to have a wide range of feelings, and we cannot help but experience all of the feelings listed above (and more). Yet some people never learn to tolerate negative emotions, and they rush to obliterate them with substance use as soon as they occur. Some people are much more sensitive than others, and the emotional pain they experience may be overwhelming. Others have a long history of responding to difficult feelings in unhealthy ways; that pattern will need to be remedied before a recovery effort is secure. A person with a history of depression, bipolar episodes, explosive anger, or shame may need targeted education and even prescribed medication to reduce the intensity and frequency of these disturbing feelings.

Positive emotions, too, can often be problematic. Exaggerated self-confidence can make addicts feel capable of coping with high-risk people, places, and things. Satisfaction and happiness, while generally desirable, can lead to complacency. Sexual arousal can lead to distraction. Indeed, many men use substances to intensify an already pleasant and stimulating emotion.

Emotions—both uncomfortable and positive—can complicate your loved one's recovery effort. I've heard many men state that they wished they could simply rid themselves of unwanted emotions, anger and loneliness in particular. Unfortunately, this is not possible. Though we may temporarily evade sorrow, grief, and other disagreeable or uncomfortable feelings, eventually we must all experience them. It is part of the human experience. We cannot escape our emotions, nor should we even try. To be emotionless or only capable of positive emotions would make us less than human.

In his best-selling book *Emotional Intelligence*, Daniel Goleman presented a paradigm for emotional literacy. Many of his original theories have been proven by later research. Emotional literacy and mastery consists of the following:[6]

- *Emotional Self-Awareness.* This is the ability to recognize emotions, name them, and understand their causes. Many men cannot name more than ten emotions (yes there are many more) and the often subtle differences between various emotions. Often, men label most of their negative feelings as either anger or sadness.

- *Managing Emotions.* This includes our ability to manage and appropriately express feelings, and our ability to delay gratification and control our impulses. Many men with substance abuse problems recognize that they are not able to manage their emotions.

- *Empathy.* Empathy is the ability to be sensitive to other people's emotions and act in a way that acknowledges their perspective. The longer a substance abuser's life is consumed by his substance use, the more strained and superficial his relationships with others become. For addicts, their true love is their drug (or drugs) of choice, and there is little need for empathy and compassion with an inert substance. Soon self-centeredness supersedes the critical emotional skill of empathy.

Part of the work of recovery, then, includes emotional awareness and management, harnessing emotions for a productive life, and increasing empathic skills. All of these abilities diminish during extended substance abuse, and some men must have to work even harder to develop these skills, as they might not have mastered them before their substance use began. A common belief in the addictions field is that people stop maturing emotionally at the age they begin to heavily use drugs and/or alcohol. I don't know if we will ever be able to empirically prove this hypothesis, but there is no doubt that many substance abusers are emotionally underdeveloped.

## CHALLENGING ONE'S THINKING

Early recovery largely requires working on behaviors; avoiding risky people, places, and things; and expanding the number of positive, drug-free activities in one's life. It also requires learning about feelings: to recognize the role negative and positive emotions play in substance use and to not instinctively respond with substance use when difficult feelings arise.

Another area for intervention is changing problematic thinking patterns. Particular sets of thoughts or ways of thinking frequently precede drug and alcohol use (for example, I need to escape; I can't deal with this unless I'm high; this is a really tough situation—I deserve to get high). These charged thoughts have a sense of urgency that can lead to drug use.

Let's consider some common patterns of problematic thoughts:[7]

- *Diminished pleasure:* "Sex is so boring without meth."

- *Entitlement:* "I busted my ass all week; I deserve a drink."

- *Feeling uncomfortable:* "How will I approach anybody at the club without some chemical assistance?"

- *Escape:* "This day has been so awful, I just need a break for a few hours."

- *Failure:* "I disappointed my boyfriend once again by not remaining sober; there's no hope for me."

- *Life will never be the same:* "Everybody I know drinks at the clubs on Friday night; as a sober person, I'll never fit in."

- *Testing control:* "I can go to parties (see friends who are users, drink, or smoke marijuana) without using" or "I can use just this one time without any problems happening."

- *What the hell:* "I screwed up again; I might as well get high."

Not surprisingly, all of the above patterns encourage a return to drug use. Here are some specific steps for changing these automatic thought patterns:

- Identify automatic thoughts—become aware of one's thinking patterns.

- Learn to reality test and not assume that automatic thoughts reflect reality.

- Learn to dispute these thoughts.

Avoiding thoughts associated with substance use is not always possible—they usually occur without conscious effort. Still, people who tend to be focused on positive goals seem to be less troubled by them. Counselors can help newly recovering people articulate and record short- and

long-term goals. Most important, they can help people in the beginning stages of recovery see possibilities *beyond* their immediate temptations and imagine a future without the discomfort they are currently
experiencing.

In recovery, people learn to pay attention to the four major components of a healthy lifestyle: diet, exercise, rest, and stress management.
With attention and support in early recovery, gay men will have more
success at incorporating all of these into their daily lives. Healthy nutrition, physical fitness, good sleep, and basic stress management all feed
each other. When we get enough exercise, we sleep better and feel less
stressed; when we eat well, we maintain a reasonable weight; when we
get a good night's sleep, we feel less stressed during the day. It's impossible to underestimate how important these four lifestyle considerations
are to continued recovery.

::

His life did not become unmanageable overnight, and most likely not
even after several months. Problems stemming from substance use
amass over time, possibly with even years of use. To expect these problems to quickly disappear and all aspects of his lifestyle to immediately
change is absurd. Many in the treatment and counseling fields warn that
it takes the same amount of time to correct a life as it did to damage it. If,
for example, your life became unmanageable over a period of three years,
you can expect that it will take you about three years to regain control
and order.

Maintaining abstinence is more difficult than simply promising himself and others that he will no longer use drugs. After all, he probably did
that before many times, and the end result was failure. Early recovery is a
process of making the changes necessary to maintain abstinence. Counselors are one of many support systems that will help him learn and practice new behaviors.

## CHAPTER SEVEN

# TWELVE STEP PROGRAMS

*When I was at the NTA [Narcotics Treatment Administration], I estab-
lished an informal ex-addict advisory group of 10 clean addicts who
worked for NTA as counselors or in other roles. They were inspiring
and contributed greatly to NTA's success. Years later, I encountered
one of these ex-addict advisors and asked him about the other group
members. "All dead," was his report. I was puzzled when he told me
that most had died. . . . I asked, "Why are you alive and they are dead?"
His response shaped my thinking forever after: "I went to AA and Narcotics Anonymous (NA) meetings, and they didn't."*
          —Robert DuPont, founding director, National Institute on Drug Abuse

MOST PEOPLE WHO ARE TRYING TO END OR REDUCE their substance use are
advised to attend Twelve Step meetings, but other interventions exist as
well. In general, the more support one gets, the better the results. Four
types of support are the most successful, and the combination of all four
offers the best outcome. I urge anyone attempting recovery to consider
all of these options in early recovery:

1. *Twelve Step meetings or some type of group support.* Those struggling with substance use problems need the wisdom and support
   of others who have traveled the same roads. The Twelve Step approach is the best-known type of mutual-help support group, but
   there are many others as well.

2. *Psychiatric support.* Fifty percent of people with substance abuse
   problems are also dealing with a psychological problem that

existed before they began using substances. For these people, maintaining psychiatric stability is absolutely essential. Far too often I have seen men stop taking their prescription medications once they began to feel better, only to then see them experience a rebound of unwanted symptoms. Substance use quickly followed.

3. *Counseling.* People who attend some form of counseling tend to do better in recovery. It's difficult to untangle some problems without help; in really difficult times we can all benefit from the guidance of professionals.

4. *Couples and family counseling.* Couples and family counseling, addressed in chapters 4 and 11, is one of the most underused interventions for substance abuse, even though we have known for years that drug abuse affects the whole family. How family members respond can be a motivating factor for continued use or a shocking wake-up call to action. Couples and family counseling is no longer a peripheral treatment but rather an essential part of a recovery effort.

I strongly advise all of the men I work with to try a Twelve Step approach to recovery, and since I live in a large metropolitan area with a number of gay- and bi-friendly meetings, I am always prepared to hand out a list of available meetings. Even more, I urge them to keep going to meetings several times a week, even if they don't initially like them. The support and education they get through these meetings can be positive turning points for men in early recovery. A man may never attend another Twelve Step meeting after early recovery, or meetings may become a foundation for a drug-free life. If he can attend a Twelve Step meeting that is safe for him, then urge him to try it. Unfortunately, finding such a meeting may be impossible for some gay men.

Just two decades ago, Twelve Step meetings were the only intervention available for a drug addiction. If you needed inpatient treatment, most of the program's curriculum was likely Twelve Step based. There were workbooks, videos, and an abundance of staff members all teaching the need for this approach. The Twelve Steps ruled the recovery scene, and the approach had (and continues to have) a remarkable track record. Without a doubt, Twelve Step groups such as NA (Narcotics Anonymous) and AA (Alcoholics Anonymous) have helped millions of people, and not just those from the United States. You can attend an international Narcotics Anonymous conference and meet people from around the globe whose lives have been improved by the principles of the Twelve Steps.

Here are the basic tenets of Twelve Step groups:

- We accept that we must end our substance use because it is causing complications, problems, and unwanted outcomes in our lives.

- We accept that our past attempts to stop or limit use have not been successful.

- We give up the belief that "this time it will be different" when we use our preferred drug(s).

- We surrender our belief in our own willpower and self-reliance to end our substance use.

If a man acknowledges that his current substance use has become compulsive and out of control, that he cannot stop substance use on his own, that it is causing havoc in his life, *and* that a group of people dealing with the very same issue may offer the knowledge and experience to help him with this problem, then a Twelve Step group is an option for him to explore.

## THE SPIRITUAL ISSUE

When you broach the possibility of Twelve Step meetings with your client or loved one, be prepared for at least hesitation if not outright refusal. In my own work, I repeatedly hear two legitimate concerns from gay men regarding the Twelve Step approach. The first is that many have ambivalence, if not outright aversion, toward any form of religious or spiritual practice, a critical part of the Twelve Steps. Indeed, the second and third Steps ask participants to believe that a Power greater than themselves could restore them to sanity, and to turn their will and life over to the care of this Power.

Most gay men have been taught that homosexuality is a sin and that having same-sex desires (and even worse, same-sex sexual activity) is a slap in the face of God. As a result, and for good reason, they may have distanced themselves from religion eons ago. Even if their spiritual backgrounds are not fringed with accounts of hell and eternal suffering, they may have simply given up on a belief in a Higher Power based on their experiences of the world. For those with an avowed and steadfast aversion to spiritual or religious practices, traditional Twelve Step groups may ultimately not be the best intervention.

While many supporters attest to the secular nature of the Steps, an expanding number of lawsuits on the constitutionality of mandated Twelve Step participation for those in the legal system have determined that they are indeed religious in nature and practice. If one is deeply uncomfortable with any organized religion, that discomfort may also include traditional Twelve Step groups and their procedures. In such cases, instead of looking for well-known Twelve Step groups such as AA, NA, or CA (Cocaine Anonymous), try to find one or both of the following secular support groups:

- Secular Organizations for Sobriety (SOS). SOS takes a reasonable, secular approach to recovery and maintains that sobriety is a separate issue from religion or spirituality. SOS credits the individual for achieving and maintaining his or her own sobriety, without reliance on any "Higher Power."

- Self-Management and Recovery Training (SMART). SMART is an international nonprofit organization that offers free, self-empowering, science-based mutual help groups for abstaining from any substance or activity addiction. SMART Recovery has a scientific foundation, not a spiritual one.

In spite of the (albeit limited) availability of these two secular organizations, most men will opt for a traditional Twelve Step program. And for those at least open to spiritual work, even if they have doubts, traditional Twelve Step groups may be invaluable. For those who are uncertain about the spiritual nature of the Twelve Steps, I suggest that in the early days of recovery, they put the entire spiritual matter aside. Going to meetings, building a positive support system, and listening to the experiences and suggestions of others who have been in the same situation are all far more important than arguing about whether a god does or does not exist.

Others in the room have these same doubts, and many still question whether a Higher Power can truly exist. So he won't be alone. As he becomes more cemented in the traditions, routines, and principles of the Twelve Steps, he will learn that reliance on a Higher Power can take on many forms. Father Leo Booth, author of *When God Becomes a Drug: Understand-*

ing *Religious Addiction and Religious Abuse,* has written extensively about spirituality and the gay community. He counsels that the most important goal for gay men is to identify the damaging messages they heard during childhood regarding God and homosexuality. He writes that by identifying these beliefs, he helps sexual minorities confront the origins of their sexual shame and instead develop spiritual empowerment. Rather than interpreting scripture as unchanging and "written in stone," he asks sexual minorities to consider scripture's implications in the modern world, promotes the questioning of authority, decreases rigid black-and-white thinking, and, ultimately, suggests that they take responsibility for their own lives. He also urges family members and helping professionals to examine their own religious beliefs about God and how they might affect their work with sexual minorities.

Finally, if as a helping professional you are unable to work through your own spiritual issues regarding sexual minorities, then, by all means, refer them to somebody who has already done this introspective work.[1]

Many in Twelve Steps groups who doubt the existence of a Higher Power in spiritual terms nevertheless accept the power of the group. "A power greater than ourselves" does not necessarily have to be a spiritual deity. According to the book *Narcotics Anonymous,* "At some point, we realized that we needed the help of some Power greater than our addiction. Our understanding of a Higher Power is up to us. No one is going to decide for us. We can call it the group, the program, or we can call it God. The only suggested guidelines are that this Power be loving, caring, and greater than ourselves."[2]

The Twelve Steps ask that he stop relying on himself for recovery; he needs to give up the belief that he can succeed through willpower and determination. Rather, he can find success by simply reaching out to other people for help, guidance, and support. As he progresses in the Twelve Steps, he may experience a spiritual enlightenment or remain a steadfast atheist or agnostic. Either way is okay. What matters is that he works with his new support group on his recovery goals.

## THE CHALLENGES OF MEETINGS

The second oft-stated dislike by gay men is related to the dynamics of Twelve Step meetings. And I agree that gay men need to be cautious in their approach to meetings. Always remember that Twelve Step groups are made up of people, and as such they have the same complexities, problems, and potential that exist when any group of people comes together.

One disadvantage to meetings is that many people who achieved their recovery through NA, AA, or related groups may be reluctant to accept new scientific findings about addiction. While Twelve Step organizations seem to embrace science at the national level, down in the trenches—in the clubhouses and individual meetings throughout the country, those places where the real action happens—the response to new science-based explanations on the origins of addiction, and the best ways to recover from those addictions, has been less than welcoming.

For example, a patient wrote his physician a letter asking about the advice he received at Twelve Step meetings. He wrote,

> I believe that Alcoholics Anonymous saved my life, and has also saved the life of my partner Chet. Please understand—I have all the respect in the world for AA, NA and other 12 Step programs. However, we are having a terrible time with one issue. Chet is HIV+ and also struggles with severe anxiety and mood swings. Right now he is doing very well under the care of several physicians, and he takes many medications: anti-retrovirals, anti-depressants, a statin to lower cholesterol, and injectable migraine medication to use when a headache strikes. He takes all these medications as prescribed by his doctors and has never abused them. At least once a week, he is talking with a member of AA or NA who tells him that he is "not really sober" and that taking pills will cause him to relapse. We have friends who have been told the same thing, that AA or NA "doesn't approve" of taking any medications, and I have seen at least one person who got very sick and had to be hospitalized because someone at a 12 Step meeting told him he should stop taking the medication his psychiatrist prescribed for his bipolar disorder. What does AA really say about taking medications?

In response, the doctor told his patient, "Officially, Alcoholics Anonymous *has no opinion on taking medication* because, according to Tradition Ten, *AA has no opinion on outside issues*, and this is an outside issue. However, members of AA *do* have lots of opinions about this issue and some do not hesitate to share them with other members, newcomers, sponsees, etc. As you have noticed, some of them attribute their private opinions to AA or NA."[3]

When people unfamiliar with, or opposed to, changes in addictions treatment are allowed to have the pulpit, it may become a bully pulpit in which any other approaches are arrogantly disregarded or mocked. I have personally attended Twelve Step meetings—one in a formal treatment setting and the other in a gay community center—in which participants were told to avoid using psychiatric medications in recovery and that sustained recovery is impossible without practicing the Twelve Steps. Neither of these sentiments accurately depicts the principles of AA and related groups, but such messages may nonetheless be intimidating and disturbing to new members.

*There is no single approach to drug abuse and addiction that supersedes others in importance, and all can complement each other to obtain a synergistic effect.* Or, as AA cofounder Bill Wilson stated, "The roads to recovery are many." Even so, a person may encounter reservations—if not outright contempt—for any method of recovery that strays from the standard Twelve Step principles.

Another challenge is that some people rely on Twelve Step principles to a fault. For example, my clinical work involves leading groups for gay men at all phases in the recovery process. For some, this is their first treatment experience. Others have relapsed many times, sometimes after years of treatment, and others after just a few months of clean time. I throw out some common relapse scenarios to the assembled men and ask them how they would respond to the risk:

"It's Friday night and you've just been paid. Your check is in your hand. How would you handle it?"

Before the question is even out of my mouth, members are speaking over each other to give an answer.

"Call my sponsor."

I try another problem: "Your lover breaks up with you suddenly by telling you he is not happy in your relationship. How would you handle this?"

Again there is a chorus: "Call my sponsor and get to a [Twelve Step] meeting."

"How would you handle running into friends who invite you to join them for a drink or for some other substance you're attempting to stay away from?"

"Call my sponsor and get to a meeting right away."

"You see a poster for an upcoming circuit party, and you suddenly find yourself craving methamphetamine and hot sex. How would you handle it?"

Okay readers, you have one guess; what do you think the response is? You're right: Call my sponsor and attend a meeting.

I hope by now you're seeing one of the unintended challenges to working within a Twelve Step format. For every problem, the solution is typically the same: Call a sponsor and attend a meeting. Yet for each problem I presented to group members above, other courses of action would have been appropriate as well. However, when I—typically in frustration—tell these men that for the remainder of the group their answers cannot involve calling a sponsor or attending a NA or AA group, I am met with stony silence. These are often very intelligent men with professional backgrounds, yet they are stumped to come up with workable and, even better, proactive solutions to the problems. Even the authors of *Accepting Ourselves and Others*, a self-help text on recovery for gay men and lesbian women (a text that wholeheartedly embraces the Twelve Step philosophy), clearly state that it is not a cure-all for all one's problems.

Another unfortunate but common problem is that some meetings for gay and bisexual men are cruisier than the local bar. Even in meetings not specifically catering to gay men but rather open to anybody, closeted men will attend hoping to scout a man who seems desperate enough to trade sex for money and/or drugs. I even know of men who pretend to have a substance abuse problem—they even shamelessly introduce themselves as addicts—with the sole intent of meeting a young man down on his luck who would be willing to engage in sexual activity for a little cash, some drugs, and likely the combination of the two. I have worked with many men in their early days of rebuilding their lives who relapsed after meeting another man at a NA or AA meeting. But I don't want to stereotype gay men. Women—especially young and attractive women—likewise report a surplus of seemingly sincere men who are more than willing to minister to their needs at NA and AA meetings. This disguise of concern and help crumbles quickly, however, and their true intentions—typically of the sexual nature—become evident. Recovery and sex do mix, but NA/AA meetings are not the places for hooking up with someone.

Finally, the popular Twelve Step slogan "Keep coming back. It'll work if you work it" minimizes the day-to-day complexities that people in recovery experience. I have seen people go back to Twelve Step meetings many, many times, often struggling for years and wondering why other men and women in the room are finding success while they themselves stay mired in their addiction. Well-meaning Twelve Step members and sponsors tell them that they need to "work the program" even more.

Is it possible, though, that some people need more than the Twelve Steps can offer? Do they have an underlying mental health condition (such as depression, anxiety, or unresolved trauma) that needs to be addressed in a clinical setting? Or do they have unaddressed physical problems (chronic pain and insomnia tend to be the most common) that do not find a viable remedy in a Twelve Step meeting room? Attendance at meetings will not necessarily resolve physical and psychological concerns.

Twelve Step programs and philosophies have performed an incredible service to an untold number of addicts, but they are unable to offer much help for another untold number of people. For some, the Steps are simply not quite right, and not enough.

## GETTING STARTED

In spite of the spiritual reservations and troublesome dynamics that occur in meetings, I still suggest gay men give Twelve Step programs a sincere try. Meetings are open to anybody who has a substance use problem, but as the name of each group suggests, each one focuses on one problem over the other. AA meetings prefer that members speak about alcohol issues, and CA meetings prefer that the dialogue center on cocaine. NA tends to be more encompassing and allows members to voice their challenges with any drug of abuse. Anybody with a substance abuse issue is welcome at all of these groups, but there is an expectation that the focus will remain on the eponymous drug. Still, some people have a strong preference for AA meetings, even if alcohol is not their primary problem. Others feel just as strongly about NA.

If your loved one or client is unable to find a meeting designed specifically for gay men or even one that is open to the encompassing queer community (this problem is more likely if he doesn't live in or near an urban area), he will have to rely on community meetings. Suggest to your client or loved one that he pick up the phone book, get online, or call the hotlines for these organizations. Most Twelve Step groups offer different types of meetings, and I suggest that he try several. Speaker meetings are those in which a person in recovery shares his or her story. Step meetings focus on one of the Twelve Steps for the entire meeting. Open meetings are those in which anybody can share. After he attends one meeting, he will learn about the plethora of options out there.

One doesn't often hear derogatory comments about African Americans, Latinos, Asians, or other ethnic minorities in Twelve Step meetings, but because gay men are often invisible and many people can't believe that there might be one (or more) in the assembled group, it is sometimes considered safe to belittle them. Still, it is highly unlikely that he will attend a meeting in which homo-hatred is blaringly obvious. No one will stand up in a meeting and state "I hate gays" or "Gays are not welcome here." To do so would be an egregious action so contrary to Twelve Step principles that even the most stoic member would be shocked into action.

If such an incident ever does happen (and again this is extremely unlikely), what follows will indicate whether the group is safe and appropriate for him. Others in the room will sit quietly and listen; it is tradition not to "cross talk," to interrupt while another member is sharing. If another member then takes his or her turn and thanks the original speaker for his story but then gently, non-accusingly, and without confrontation reminds the participants that the meeting is open to everybody and that the only requirement is a desire to end substance use, this second speaker in effect made it clear that gay men are welcome.

Gay men, accustomed to cautiously scanning their surroundings to ensure their safety, have learned to pick up cues that signal a welcoming or dangerous environment, and I coach them to let that "sixth sense" guide them in determining the safety of meetings. For some gay men this sense, after years of negative treatment and even overt physical and mental torment, has become too sensitive, perceiving a threat when there is none and detecting an implied homo-hatred in even the most benign circumstances.

If during a meeting nobody corrects the members spewing heterosexist vitriol either firmly or indirectly, he should find another meeting. If he doesn't find a group that feels comfortable to him, his chances of becoming a dropout statistic are astronomical. And don't for a minute think he won't encounter heterosexism and homo-hatred in even all-gay male meetings. Some gay men will verbalize their own internalized homophobia and, as such, a tragic hatred of themselves. These are the men whose relentless shame over their own identity contributed to both the development and continued fueling of their substance abuse issues. One of the primary reasons Twelve Step self-help groups work is that, by sharing their stories, substance abusers can recognize what pitfalls and successes they have in common with others. They can learn from each other.

The general recommendation is to attend six meetings before deciding if the group will be beneficial, unless of course the group is so heterosexist that continued attendance could only lead to mental health and possible safety risks.

---

### SIGNS OF A HEALTHY TWELVE STEP GROUP

How do you know if a particular Twelve Step group is healthy? Here are some telltale signs that Patrick Carnes identified in his book *Facing the Shadow:*[4]

- Strong regular attendance.

- Members take responsibility for leadership positions.

- Each week, someone in the group takes responsibility for presenting either a Step or a topic.

- The Step presentations or topic presentations are prepared and thoughtful.

- There is a well-understood and supported process for welcoming newcomers.

- The group has strong ties with a codependency support group.

- There is a group life outside of the meeting in the form of regular meals together, workshops, or retreats.

- Periodically—at least every quarter—the group stops to do a "group conscience," which means the members hold an extended discussion about how the group is doing.

- Leadership and "jobs" in the group rotate regularly.

- There is a steady influx of new persons.

- There is steady attendance of veterans who have successful sobriety.

Gay men who are unable to find a local Twelve Step meeting specifically for gay men should determine if the setting of available meetings
can help them to do the following: build a new support system, establish
a relationship with a loving Higher Power (with no implication that their
sexuality is wrong and sinful), become increasingly honest and open in
their sharing and disclosure, and develop full and meaningful lives. Most
important, a Twelve Step meeting that is healthy for gay men should
never increase their internalized heterosexism and shame.[5]

Remember, despite the claims of other members who seem to know
everything, the only requirement to be a Twelve Step member is the desire to stop drug use. There is no need to call oneself an addict, to recite
the recovery prayer, to reveal one's sexual orientation, or even to attend
on a regular basis (keeping in mind that frequent attendance is connected with higher levels of success). Nor does attending a meeting mean
that a person has to commit to a lifetime—or even a week's worth—of abstinence. All he needs to do is admit that he wants to stop for today. He
takes responsibility for his recovery on a daily basis.

## FINDING LONG-TERM SUCCESS WITH THE STEPS

Too many gay men enter Twelve Step meetings focused on what makes
them different from the other addicts in attendance; they spend much
of the group time comparing themselves to others' education, financial
circumstances, background, spirituality, and even ethnicity. They try to
convince themselves that they are unique and that the others could not
possibly understand their experiences. This is egotism at its worst: I am
so different that nobody could comprehend my problems. Focusing on
differences in this way distracts the new member from seeing how all of
the individuals in the room are alike. A better approach is to enter each
Twelve Step meeting with an eye for what is shared rather than what is
not, or, in the words of AA, "identify, don't compare." Everybody in that
room has some form of substance use problem.

Long-term success with the Twelve Steps entails more than sitting
quietly in the meeting room several times a week. Instead, it requires getting active and making a commitment to positive change in life. First, he
has to participate in meetings. Second, he can volunteer to perform a task
such as setting up the meeting or cleaning up afterward, making coffee,

and attending NA/AA socials. He should also exchange phone numbers with other members. This is a long-held AA and NA tradition, so he may return home with several phone numbers from people he has just met. Sure, some of these strangers could be those cretins who prey on men early in recovery, but more likely they are well-intentioned people doing just what is expected of them in the Twelve Step tradition. If a person gives out his number, he expects it to be used. He can call this individual (or individuals, as he will likely receive more than one phone number) whenever he has a craving or urge to use drugs again, is feeling unpleasant emotions, or is overwhelmed by life's problems.

## SPONSORS

At some point, the possibility of a sponsor arises. This is one of the oldest traditions in Twelve Step programs. Sponsors are other Twelve Step members, usually with more experience, who volunteer their available time twenty-four hours a day to offer advice, solace, and support. They also provide basic information on the Twelve Steps and its traditions, and help new members get more active in the group. Sponsors are not meant to be counselors or therapists, but instead use their own recovery experiences—both the good and the bad—to guide newly recovering people through their recovery. Many people take on a series of temporary sponsors until they find the one who is the most perfect fit.

For straight men and women, the standard suggestion is to choose a sponsor of the same sex to minimize romantic attraction (which can derail or at least complicate the relationship). But what if you're a gay male? Do you opt for a female sponsor? Do you opt for a straight male sponsor? How about a lesbian sponsor? The preferred solution is to avoid sponsorship by another gay man, even if you are not attracted to him. Sexual urges can surface on either man's part, and too often this detracts from the intended focus of the collaboration. Of course, in some situations other gay men are the only available options for sponsors; if that's the case, the sponsor and sponsee should address the issue of sexual and romantic attraction early on in their relationship. So let's end this discussion with a recommendation with which few people would disagree: If he has a romantic attraction and/or sexual relationship with his sponsor, it's time to find a new sponsor.

## MODERATION AND THE TWELVE STEPS

What about moderation and controlled substance use? This is what many gay male substance abusers are seeking in the long term. Indeed, many people enter Twelve Steps meetings hoping to hear they can use in moderation, and they may even experiment to find out if this is true. Some will be successful, while others will not. The Twelve Steps do not ask for a lifetime commitment to abstinence but rather a "one day at a time" approach. All that is asked is that one stay clean today and commit to do so on a daily basis. AA and related groups will not look askance if those purposefully intent on moderation in substance use attend quietly. If, however, one repeatedly promotes moderation in use to a room of individuals desiring abstinence, expect a backlash.

::

There is so much more about Twelve Steps groups that simply cannot be described in this brief chapter. For instance, we have only examined the first three of the Twelve Steps. The only way his questions will be answered is to go out and attend a meeting. His initial confusion will dissipate as he becomes more familiar with the process and protocol.

In his best-selling book *Healing the Addicted Brain*, Harold Urschel offers an extremely important reason for trying a Twelve Step approach: "Due to financial considerations, most addiction treatment programs only last four to eight weeks. This may sound like a long time when you enter into a program, but it is impossible to completely overcome addiction in one or two months—even six months or a year. Addiction is a lifelong chronic disease that requires lifelong commitment. Unless you're prepared to pay for years or decades of treatment, the only place to go for that kind of continual care is AA."[6]

Many people who enter a Twelve Step program adopt it as a lifestyle; indeed the Steps themselves are guidelines for completely renovating one's life. Others, though, use it as a temporary means to become clean and sober and then move on. In my work, I find that the number of gay men who make substantial improvements with their substance abuse problems by following Twelve Step principles, meetings, and sponsorship is dwarfed by those for whom they are not an option. Most gay men will not or cannot make use of this most common recommendation for support in recovery from substance abuse. Whatever their reasons—time constraints, distance, a lack of gay-friendly meetings, a dislike of groups, antipathy toward some of the principle tenets of these meetings—most gay men will not use them as the primary route for their recovery. And if they do try this well-known route, most will stop after several months.

In the end, if your loved one or client sincerely does not want to attend meetings, declines to participate in a Twelve Step approach or even a more secular program, or simply cannot attend due to logistical or safety reasons, it really is okay. He can make positive changes even if he does shun this most recognized intervention. That is what the rest of this book is about—options. I still recommend that he try it though, since it complements other available interventions.

## CHAPTER EIGHT

# RELAPSE

IF ENDING SUBSTANCE USE WERE EASY, we wouldn't need hundreds of self-help books on the topic. Indeed, staying abstinent from alcohol and other drugs is far more difficult than many imagine. This is why most of the work in the early stages of recovery focuses solely on staying clean and dry. Only when a man has gained some time being drug free can he begin to make permanent changes in his life, even if, paradoxically, his goal is controlled use. Abstinence is difficult for many men to maintain; they might stop substance use for several weeks or even months and then suddenly and often inexplicably find themselves using once again. Why does this happen? What can these men do to stay on course? Answering these questions is the focus of this chapter.

Some readers may think I am being an apologist by presenting the many challenges gay men face in recovery. I am trying to be realistic. I can't begin to describe how difficult it will be for some gay men to give up or reduce their substance use; relapse is more likely than not. But I am not asking you to feel sorry for him, or have low expectations for him if you are his counselor; after all he cannot relapse if he doesn't pick up his substance or substances of choice. That *is* in his control. It is *his* recovery effort, and you are a merely a supporting actor on the stage with him.

## THE CHALLENGE OF CHANGE

Some of the top New Year's resolutions are to get out of debt, quit smoking, and create more quality time in one's life. From your own experience, though, how many of these resolutions actually last more than a few months? By June, less than half have maintained their promise, and a year later, less than 10 percent are successful. Let's get even more spe cific: The most common New Year's Eve resolution is to lose weight (and get into shape). We all recognize that a lack of physical exercise is bad for our health; we can even quote health experts' recommendations for physical activity. We may be dissatisfied with our body, our health, and even our inability to walk up a flight of stairs without becoming winded. Yet, in spite of promises to exercise every day and even a gallant begin- ning by joining a health club, within several months almost all of us have "relapsed" back to our sedentary lifestyles. And this includes gay men, in spite of popular depictions of them as disciplined gym attendees.

One of the most fascinating (though horrid) examples of diet relapse involves men and women who underwent major heart surgery. In the book *Change or Die*, Dr. Edward Miller, dean of the medical school at Johns Hopkins University, tells stories that illustrate how very difficult change is. He describes "patients whose arteries are so clogged that any kind of exertion is terribly painful for them. It hurts too much to take a long walk. It hurts too much to make love. So surgeons have to im- plant pieces of plastic to prop open their arteries, or remove veins from their legs to stitch near the heart so that blood can bypass the blocked passages. The procedures are traumatic and expensive—they cost more than $100,000. More than one and a half million people every year in the United States undergo coronary bypass graft or angioplasty surgery at a total price of around $60 billion."[1]

These patients *had to* begin investing in a healthier lifestyle—change how they eat and how active they are, manage their stress better, stop smoking; this was the only sure way to avoid another bypass and pre- vent early death. Many of these patients were in deplorable condition before the surgery and many would have died were it unavailable. From a period of a few weeks to several months after the surgery, they fas- tidiously followed the protocol. But after two years, *90 percent had re- verted back to their original unhealthy lifestyle*. A related study found that many patients with pre-existing heart disease who were prescribed statins (drugs that reduce the risk of heart attack and death in patients with proven coronary artery disease) stopped taking pills after the first two months. One year later, only one-fifth were taking the medication even though they were supposed to take them the rest of their lives.

Efforts to end or reduce substance use can have as little success as *any other change effort in our lives*. Anyone with a drug addiction can recite a litany of problems and complications caused by substance use: health issues, lost jobs, financial stress, and strained relationships with the people who love them. But just like Dr. Miller's patients above, consequences—even those that risk our very lives—are not enough to dissuade a gradual return to unhealthy habits. Fear may be a great motivator to begin a behavior change, but it is not potent enough to keep one going through the difficult stages of the change process.

## RELAPSE AND SUBSTANCE USE

The definition of addiction from the National Institute on Drug Abuse includes relapse as one of its basic characteristics: "Addiction is a chronic, relapsing brain disease that is characterized by compulsive drug seeking and use, despite harmful consequences."[2] Most addicts discover that their staunch commitment to slow down or stop their drug use tends to fade over time. What began as one allowable night of partying each month eventually progressed to going out once or twice a week. While it would undoubtedly be best if he could keep his first promise to cut down or stop using alcohol and other drugs completely throughout his life, this is simply a rare occurrence. Relapse happens, and it will happen to almost everyone who attempts to change their drug use patterns.

Many people think relapses occur because of a lack of willpower, that a person simply wasn't strong enough in the face of temptation. While this explanation makes sense if you're not aware of the new scientific findings on addiction, or if you still believe the archaic model that describes addiction as a moral deficiency, in reality, relapse is far more complicated and nuanced.

It is crucial for clinicians and other helping professionals to understand and internalize that relapse is common and complex. Why? Because their clients who have relapsed—gay or straight, male or female—are very likely struggling with strong feelings of personal weakness. Helping professionals can help reduce their clients' feelings of shame by teaching them about the complexity of relapse. Although relapse may look simple (they returned to substance abuse), it occurs due to a convergence of many underlying factors—factors that are different for everybody.

## Positive Emotions

One of the most frustrating experiences I regularly encounter in substance abuse inpatient treatment settings is the farewell speech a patient gives on his last day of treatment. By the time he reaches this graduation, he is likely ending a thirty-day period devoted to treatment, including educational groups, individual counseling, and NA/AA groups on a daily basis. As he sits in the community room in the morning hours surrounded by other men who are not yet ready to leave, he receives heartfelt congratulations from staff and peers. He offers a review of his treatment experience, both the good and bad over the past thirty days. He singles out specific staff and peers for accolades, and often slyly hints at a private joke that causes some of the assembled men in the room to quietly laugh. Typically this refers to surreptitious sexual activity that occurred and was not noticed by the staff.

These farewell speeches end with a call for peers to keep moving forward in their own efforts and a description of how good he himself feels right in the present moment. He hopes that all those in the room will feel just as positive, enthusiastic, and motivated as he does when it is their turn to leave. He can't believe how much drug and/or alcohol use had affected him until his head was clear and he saw the trail of consequences and repercussions. At this point many men become tearful. The journey ahead seems so straightforward, unambiguous, and clear. Yes. He recognizes the relapse dangers awaiting him when he returns to his home environment. Although there are innumerable stressors that he could not ease during his thirty days of treatment, with his new perspective on his life and his drug problem, nothing seems insurmountable. *The chance that this man—the same person now filled with passion for recovery on his last day of treatment—will return to substance abuse within six months is remarkably high.* Within one year of leaving treatment, the odds are definitely stacked against him.

I tell all men who seek help for drug problems that their feelings on the last day of treatment—passion, enthusiasm, hope, and often joy— have absolutely no bearing on how well they will fare with efforts at long-term recovery. The joy of completing treatment—of having addressed a litany of problems that desperately needed intervention, sometimes for years—cannot but help lead even the most reticent and stolid man to feel positive about himself. But again, feeling positive about oneself does not automatically translate into success with one's goals for recovery, whether those goals are for reducing or eradicating drug use. Sure, I would rather a man leave treatment feeling better than when he came in, and if he continued to feel deeply depressed and anxious while still in treatment, I would be uncomfortable ending that treatment (although his insurance might not pay for him to stay any longer, and he might have to pay out of pocket). But too many people mistakenly believe that their positive feelings and aspirations foretell success. I am personally astounded that this issue receives so little attention, as I consider it one of the fundamental and most common errors in early treatment.

## Prefeeling

It's difficult to know how we will feel about a certain event in our lives until we're actually facing it. Consider how Harvard psychology professor Daniel Gilbert views this experience:

> Have you ever wondered why you often make commitments that you deeply regret when the moment to fulfill them arrives? We all do this, of course. We agree to babysit the nephews and nieces next month, and we look forward to that obligation even as we jot it in our diary. Then, when it actually comes time to buy the Happy Meals, set up the Barbie playset, hide the bong, and ignore the fact that the NBA playoffs are on at one o'clock, we wonder what we were thinking . . . we find it particularly difficult to imagine that we will ever think, want, or feel differently than we do now. Teenagers get tattoos because they are confident that DEATH ROCKS will always be an appealing motto, new mothers abandon a promising law career because they are confident that being at home with their children will always be a rewarding job, and smokers who have just finished a cigarette are confident for at least five minutes that they can easily quit and their resolve will not diminish with the nicotine in their bloodstreams.[3]

Gilbert uses the word "prefeeling" to describe predicting the amount of emotion we will experience from a future event, in this case a life without drug use. The men graduating from my program who are so obviously bursting with pride over their early accomplishments in recovery cannot help but believe that they will feel the same way in the future.

But we simply cannot accurately predict our feelings; all of us have experienced the error of prefeeling even if we have never touched a drug in our lives.

I am much more comfortable when someone graduating from treatment announces that though he might be feeling great today and hopes to feel this motivated and positive in the near future, he recognizes that emotions can change quickly and that these positive feelings may be gone in a flash. Every addiction professional has seen even the most motivated and excited individual relapse just twenty-four hours after acclaiming the joys of a drug-free life. Emotions change. Motivation changes. Commitment changes. Fortunately, the reverse also holds true: people who are doubtful and even ambivalent about a drug-free life can quickly turn into the most committed and zealous adherents of their new lifestyle.

Making predictions about our future emotional state based on how we are feeling today has absolutely no bearing on how we will feel tomorrow, next week, and several months in the future. The longer we look into the future, the less realistic today's appraisal will be.

## The Screw 'Ems

The fleeting nature of our emotions holds true for negative as well as positive emotions. Whether you have a drug problem or not, people have bad days and even bad weeks. Maybe we can identify the root(s) to our negative state or maybe we simply woke up on the wrong side of bed. People with substance abuse problems do not handle negative emotions very well, and they often cope by rushing to the comfort of their drug or drugs of choice. They forget that no matter how angry or disappointed they may be at their boss, lover, mother, etc., and no matter how justified they think their feelings are, those feelings will soon pass and exert far less influence over their behavior. Still, too many addicts seek immediate gratification for any negative emotion.

One particular negative mind-set is often referred to as the "screw 'ems" by the men I work with. When they enter this state, they simply stop caring about recovery. As Richard S. Sandor describes it in *Thinking Simply about Addiction: A Handbook for Recovery*,

> People who relapse as a result of not caring . . . know very well that
> 'there is no such thing as one' but are so beside themselves with grief,

fear, shame, rage, or boredom that they simply can't stand it. If they
think about it at all, their thoughts go something like this: "If this is how
it feels to be sober, the hell with it. I was just as miserable when I was
drinking; at least then I had a little relief."[4]

The combination of low tolerance for negative emotions and unrealistic expectations causes many gay men to falter when their visions of
recovery do not pan out. So what are unrealistic expectations? It is unrealistic for them to think that their problems will miraculously resolve
quickly, that those who care for them should now accept them at face
value and immediately trust them again, and that life should be a steady
progression upwards without setbacks, disasters, or traumas. The "screw
'ems" can arise anytime in recovery and, without the active support of
others, often lead to a relapse.

## Seemingly Unimportant Decisions

Hypnosis works. It certainly doesn't work to the same degree for everybody, and some people can barely enter a trance state while others can do
so in mere seconds. My work with this latter group has shaped much of
my clinical perspective. One common interaction used in hypnosis training involves the hypnotist giving a post-hypnotic suggestion to a person to open and close a window every time the hypnotist yawns. When
this person awakens from the trance, all that he remembers is a comfortable sleep. Yet after the trance, he still has an uncontrollable urge to go to
the window and open it whenever the hypnotist yawns. If the hypnotist
asked him why he just leapt from his chair and rushed to the nearest window, the person does not respond "you told me to do it." He has no memory of this suggestion, but he will *create* a reason for his action—most
likely that "the room is too hot" or "I need some air." We try to make sense
of our behaviors even when there is no logical explanation.

Now let's expand on the power of hypnosis. Imagine that we take
a man and lead him into a hypnotic state, but instead of directing him
to open a window or follow through on some other immediate suggestion, we tell him to stop for ice cream on his way home that evening.
Some men, upon waking from the trance and having no memory of the
directive given to them, will immediately begin craving their favorite
ice cream.

Others react in a much more intriguing way—they have no immediate desire for this treat, and if asked if they are hungry for any particular
sweet, they reply with a resounding "no." As we follow our man on the
way home, possibly even seven hours later, he stops for gas. Once he gets
to the local station, instead of paying outside at the pump as he usually
does, he heads inside for a pack of cigarettes. Now, once inside the mini-
market, he feels thirsty and decides to buy a soda. And guess what? Right
next to the drink station is a freezer displaying quarts of ice cream. Of
course he decides to purchase a quart, or maybe even two. After all, he
doesn't treat himself very often, and ice cream might be a perfect reward
as he watches television tonight.

From an outsider's perspective, we can follow the above man's pattern almost as if we were connecting the dots. A leads to B leads to C
leads to ice cream. The end has already been predetermined. But from
this same man's perspective, there is no pattern. The need for gas, then
cigarettes, then a soda, then ice cream are unrelated. He cannot recognize
that his mind has set him on a mission that it is determined to accom-
plish, even if that means following through with a seemingly unrelated
series of events.

This happens all the time with addictions, so much so that the phrase
"seemingly unimportant decisions" was developed. When I encounter
such scenarios, I am reminded of the connect-the-dots activities that my
four-year-old niece does. Even though every adult in the room can look
at the unfinished picture and see that the end product will be a teddy
bear or a doll, she is still incapable of recognizing the patterns and seems
utterly amazed when she connects the numbers together with straight
lines and ends up with a picture of something recognizable. People with
substance abuse problems act in much the same way—they are baffled
that they lapsed or relapsed and they need a lot of help to connect the
chain of events that resulted in their predicament. Upon investigation
they are dumbstruck to realize that the relapse process started hours, if
not days, earlier.

People recovering from addictions are masters at setting up a complicated web of interconnected occurrences that unyieldingly lead to substance abuse. But they then protest their innocence: "I never meant for
this to happen." "It came out of the blue." Once a man has stopped or cut
down on his drug use, his goal is to maintain this behavior, so how can
that goal be thwarted so easily?

Unexpected surprises and tragedies can, and often do, affect an addict's motivation to stay drug free (such as a parent's death, a job loss, running into a former drinking buddy he hasn't seen in years, or a hot stud comes on to him and implores him to have a drink). When such events occur, he often forgets his vows and is swept up in the moment, leading to a return to substance use. Sometimes the process leading to relapse is much more subtle—especially on the surface. He can go through the early months of recovery inadvertently and unconsciously setting himself up for relapse; each seemingly unimportant decision moves him one step closer to drug use.

Recall that addiction is a brain disease, and the brain is very good at leading us from one almost unconscious choice to another so that we become involved in events that seem accidental or fortuitous. When I lead groups for gay men in recovery, the stories they tell that reveal how little they understand of their own complicity in relapse are astounding. Many involve sex. Patrick, for example, had never had sex without drinking at least several drinks. After five weeks of abstinence, he lapsed and got drunk on a Thursday night. What was his explanation? He went to the gym, another guy came on to him, and they ended up at the other man's place, a home with a stocked bar.

Patrick claimed that this chain of events was certainly accidental. But wait. Patrick hadn't worked out at the gym for a month. On Thursday, when he was feeling pretty damn horny, he didn't go to the gym for a workout so much as for the opportunity to meet another willing male. Also, he has no alcohol at his apartment, so why didn't he bring his sex partner back to his house? Although he claims he was entirely innocent, Patrick wanted some action but knew he would be unable to perform and enjoy the experience without at least two drinks in him. His rationale *sounds* plausible, at least to himself, and at least until others point out his false reasoning.

Accidents happen. Unplanned events arise. Unforeseen high-risk scenarios can suddenly appear. But just as often—if not more often—these ostensibly accidental, unplanned, and unforeseen scenarios have been carefully mapped out and put into action with barely a conscious recognition that such a combination of events is purposefully driving a man back to drug use.

The human brain is a miraculous organ. It houses our creativity, passions, and cherished memories, as well as our dreams and aspirations. But the human brain is also the seat of depression, the source of severe mental illness such as hearing threatening and demeaning bodiless voices, the reason why some people can't overcome compulsions such as washing their hands hundreds of times daily or checking the stovetop exactly one hundred times before they leave the house. While we cannot directly control the brain's activity, the rest of the human body is under the brain's control. Science is now elaborating on just how little of our behavior is under conscious control, and addiction certainly is an example of this.

Ori and Rom Brafman's best-selling book *Sway: The Irresistible Power of Irrational Behavior* details the covert psychological forces that sabotage rational decision making. They conclude, "Living in a time when we can predict hurricanes, treat diseases with complex medical interventions, map the universe, and reap the benefits of systematized business approaches, it's easy to forget that under the surface we humans are still influenced by irrational psychological forces that can undermine a logical perspective of the world around us. The fact is, all of us are swayed at times by factors that have nothing to do with logic or reason."[5]

These covert psychological forces are most evident in circumstances involving sexual arousal and/or drug use. Fortunately, substance abusers can become even more careful in scrutinizing their plans and daily activities to determine likely outcomes. Part of the relapse prevention plan for substance abuse and addiction—indeed, any addiction, including gambling, sex, or shopping—is to monitor one's behaviors and motivations. While some relapses do occur "out of the blue," often coinciding with events that are heavy with emotion (including sexual arousal), most are planned in advance.

## Beliefs

I carry my daily multivitamin, baby aspirin, and calcium supplement in a recycled prescription vial. And, on occasion, if I have a restless night's sleep but still plan on working out at the gym later in the day, I add an "energy supplement" (one of the over-the-counter caffeine-based products) tablet into the mix. Not too long ago, at noon, half an hour before hitting the gym, I took the energy supplement. In about twenty minutes I felt a reassuring increase in alertness and enthusiasm and a brightness in mood. And as happens with me when I have caffeine, I became quite talkative and spoke to and joked with many people during the workout (some probably none too happy with my interruptions). Finally, my stamina was increased for the duration of the workout. So far there is nothing out of the ordinary in my account. However, several hours later as I prepared to down the calcium supplement with a meal, I recognized that the energy supplement was still in the vial. I was perplexed for a second until it dawned on me that what I had swallowed prior to my workout was the calcium pill, not the energy supplement. The pills looked similar but how could a calcium tablet produce the results I experienced that day in the gym? It can't—that is, unless I *believe* it can.

Most people are going to slip at least once and probably several times in their recovery efforts. When that happens, people who believe that a slip means complete failure tend to simply give up. "Why even try?" they ask themselves. They think a slip signifies a complete lack of willpower and a loss of all the progress they have made. But a "lapse" is not the same thing as a "relapse," a distinction that G. Alan Marlatt, an eminent professional in addictions treatment, confirms. A lapse is the initial use of a drug after a period of abstinence, and a relapse involves continued use after this first lapse. In his book *Healing the Addicted Brain,* Harold Urschel also discusses this difference: "There is a significant difference between a lapse and a relapse, but it's important to understand that they are points on the same continuum—and that one continuum points in one direction only, the direction of danger. A lapse is *not* okay, and it is *not* better to suffer a bunch of 'little lapses' rather than a single relapse. Neither is it true that a lapse can be ignored, while a relapse signals the end of all hope. Both lapses and relapses are warning signs that must be addressed immediately."[6]

Every week I meet at least one person whose slip led to outright relapse. Joe, for example, had achieved three years of abstinence before he succumbed to the temptation of alcohol at his sister's wedding. Afterward, as he stood outside the rented hall, he was overcome with guilt, shame, and hopelessness. At that moment, he felt like "a failure." Of course, this led to a few more drinks at the wedding and was the beginning of a two-month run of out-of-control alcohol use. The question is, was that one drink at his sister's wedding powerful enough to trigger such a relapse, or was Joe's belief system at fault? Researchers believe that the addict's belief system partially explains why someone like Joe would continue drinking after making an initial slip. People who see the all-too-common first drink or drug as an indicator of complete defeat and a permanent lack of willpower are more likely to let a momentary lapse progress into a destructive and far-reaching relapse.

*Slips in one's goals for reduced drug use or complete abstinence tend to lead to one of two beliefs: either one is a failure and can thus never succeed at recovery or, in contrast, that one really has an abundance of self-control because the slip did not lead to a complete, immediate relapse. Both thought patterns, however, ultimately lead to relapse.* A healthier approach is to recognize a slip as a mistake *and* an opportunity to learn about oneself and one's risk factors and personal high-risk scenarios; doing so seems to reduce the potential for deterioration into relapse. The fact that one's thoughts, beliefs, and predictions affect relapse offers much-needed shading to the other black-and-white belief that a lapse inescapably propels one into relapse.

## Conditioning

Drugs have such a powerful effect on the brain that an intense and overwhelming desire to use drugs can occur even years into recovery when a person is confronted by "people, places, and things" associated with past substance abuse. And this does not have to happen on a conscious level. We can understand that stumbling into a situation in which cocaine is being shared would be a difficult predicament for a former cocaine addict. But often these triggers are not so evident.

One of the experiences associated with drug use for gay men is sexual activity. For those whose sexual experiences primarily involved some type of drug use, sexual arousal by itself becomes challenging. When Marc, for example, sees an attractive man walking down the street, his first reaction is to feel physically aroused. Soon thereafter he is overcome with a craving for his past drug of choice. This is bewildering to him, and he wonders "where did this craving come from?"

## THE DANGERS OF EARLY RECOVERY

I hope these last few pages have made it clear that relapse is far more than just a failure of willpower. Our brains are wired to maintain established patterns of use, so in many ways our brains are working against us if we are trying to learn new behaviors and patterns that do not involve using drugs. Seemingly unimportant decisions, emotions, expectations, and cravings due to contact with people, places, and things once associated with drug use are just some of the triggers that can lead to relapse; there are indeed many more. Yet this does not give someone permission to simply shrug off responsibility and say "Why bother? Obviously I'm going to fail no matter what I do." Millions of people have achieved a satisfying life in spite of past histories of substance abuse and dependence, even individuals whom everybody else had given up on.

The first year of behavior change is the most risky. Research also tells us that three-quarters of relapses are preceded by one or more of the following:[7]

- Negative emotions. Any incident that triggers a gay man's internalized homophobia and shame is applicable here.

- Physical discomfort. Withdrawal and post-acute withdrawal symptoms are obvious here, but even just being tired or having a headache can be a trigger.

- Conflict with other people, especially those who are closest to the substance abuser.

- Social pressure. For example, times when the person is in a social situations in which substances are readily available or when that person wants to celebrate.

- Sexual arousal or sexual encounters—this is especially applicable to gay men.

Some men may go right for their substance of choice when they confront one of these relapse predictors. Others are able to wait it out, at least for a while. For these latter men, there are several warning signs that indicate he might be veering toward a lapse or relapse:

1. A change in attitude (particularly overconfidence or the screw 'ems) in which he no longer feels a need or desire to participate in a regimented recovery program, and he no longer sees its value.

2. A minimal effort or outright refusal to discuss thoughts or emotions.

3. Social breakdown in which he no longer meets with sober friends or when he becomes reclusive and withdrawn.

4. Evidence of schedule changes (such as sleeping later, skipping meals, or neglecting to shave).

5. Abrupt or bad decision making or difficulty making decisions.

## How to Approach Relapse

Of course you're hoping that your client or loved one will not relapse, but what should you do if he does? The most crucial suggestion I offer is to *stay calm*. And that advice holds equally true for loved ones, therapists, and partners. Recall that earlier in this chapter I referred to the power of beliefs; many individuals believe that a singular slip in their recovery proves a drug-free life is impossible, and this of course leads to a complete relapse.

If you are his partner or a family member, you may have been the recipient of his numerous promises of abstinence and even witnessed seemingly sincere efforts at this goal. Still, they all came to naught. In your eyes, his most recent relapse may be just more evidence that he can never make it. No doubt, you have every reason to be utterly frustrated. If, however, he really did seem to be making an effort, now is not the time to cast blame or criticize, but rather to problem solve.

If you are his therapist, of course you have more emotional distance and detachment in your relationship, but you may still be tempted to give up on him and to send him signals—however unconscious—that he is a failure who can never succeed at recovery.

Rather than looking at lapses and even outright relapses as failures, let's view them as learning experiences. People berate themselves endlessly when they slip in their recovery efforts, and sadly other people are just as willing to remind them that they indeed failed. Remember, a slip is defined as a brief return to a problematic behavior. And we can't learn without making mistakes. Mistakes allow a person to consider what led up to them and choose better ways for dealing with any particular situation in the future. Slips are best approached as a sign that he needs your help to review his commitment and his plans.

Jose, for example, recognized that he abuses cocaine but has no intention of abstinence. He does, however, promise that he will *only* use it on Friday nights and *only* spend fifty dollars for this drug. He accomplishes this for several weeks without a problem. Then five weeks into his commitment, he meets a muscular jock—his ideal of physical perfection—and they head back to his place for some nocturnal action. One thing leads to another, cocaine is introduced, and before long he and his new lover are both adding hundreds of dollars to the kitty and having cocaine personally delivered to his house. Jose is upset with himself not only for crashing for two days after this slip but also for spending the money he had been saving for a vacation.

In Jose's case, with your help he can now see that anonymous sex poses a risk to his recovery. Since he does not plan on giving up sex, he can now think about ways to respond to the thoughts, emotions, and behaviors that will likely accompany sexual liaisons and that can lead to a slip. Jose needs to consider what he can do differently so his sexual encounters do not cause him to break promises to himself.

A slip or relapse may be a signal that he needs to redouble his recovery efforts or acknowledge that his current plans are not working. What then needs to change? First, revisit the essentials. Does he need to join a Twelve Step group? If he has already done this, maybe he needs to consider attending more often. Could he have a co-occurring psychiatric condition? Has he expanded his range of pleasurable non-drug-related activities and friendships? Does he have too much free time? Is he taking care of himself, physically and emotionally? Getting enough rest? Is he too stressed? Continue to investigate until it's clear what changes have to be made.

What if, as his therapist, you find out that his sexual orientation and/or shame are key to his relapse? This is an opportunity for you to reinforce, for him, that his relapse is not because he is gay; his relapse may stem from specific behaviors relating to his lifestyle or even shame over his sexual identity, but it most certainly is not because he is gay. Remind him that his sexual identity does not cause substance use; for many gay substance abusers it instead comes about through living as a sexual minority in a heterosexist world.

Rather than focusing on his sexual orientation, it's better to ask these kinds of questions: What stops him from living a satisfying life as a gay man? What kind of activities is he engaging in that may be setting him up to relapse? Some of these activities may be of a sexual nature, and not all helping professionals are comfortable asking about these issues. Even if you are comfortable, such questions might very well evoke intense discomfort in him. Nonetheless, they need to asked, if not by you, then at some point by a person whom he trusts.

:   :

A relapse is a return to old habits. It may be preceded by several slips that are blithely ignored or it may seem to come out of nowhere, with no obvious starting point. However, we need to be careful with the word "obvious." Everyone is different. Some people with an addiction problem may be actively moving toward both slips and relapses through those pesky seemingly unimportant decisions. Others may simply give up and relapse when faced with stress and trauma that seems insurmountable. I have worked with many men who completely gave up their recovery efforts when they were diagnosed with HIV. Although most were able to pull themselves back together eventually, this often took months, and for some, their drug use only exacerbated their medical conditions.

I have met very few people who achieved their substance use goals on their first attempt. Remember, addiction is defined as a disease with numerous relapse episodes. Those who attend Twelve Step meetings recite "addiction is a cunning disease." Our brains are cunning in leading us back to the flood of dopamine that only drugs and alcohol can supply.

As you work with your loved one or client through his early weeks and months of recovery, keep in mind that slips are almost inevitable and relapse may well occur. "Why bother trying, then?" he may ask. Point out that we all need to bother with many efforts in our lives that are plagued by relapse. Diets and exercise regimens often falter after a few months or end prematurely. That does not mean that we cannot do better next time. Following through on even seemingly simple changes in our lives is difficult and involves making several missteps. It's no different with recovery efforts, so let's not heap so much blame on substance abuse relapse.

Returning to one's old ways and habits is simply part of the recovery process. When it happens, the sooner he catches himself, puts the self-defeating hopelessness behind him, and tries again, the more successful he will be. Nobody became an addict or substance abuser overnight, and few will become abstinent or return to moderate controlled use quickly either.

## CHAPTER NINE

# LIFELONG ABSTINENCE OR MODERATE USE?

THOUGH HIS PARENTS WERE ENRAGED when he informed them, twenty-seven-year-old Brandon had decided not to end his drug use but instead to cut down to a more manageable level. His goal was to consume no more than two drinks per day and to use cocaine only once a week. He did, however, want to stop smoking marijuana for now. Despite the many problems his substance use produced in his life and the lives of his family, he was not ready to quit completely. He believed he could manage his drug use. Obviously, his parents were upset and deeply wounded; Brandon had put them through hell for several years.

How would you handle such an announcement? Some men simply refuse to give up all substance use; they'll cut back or forgo one or two substances from their wider assortment of drug use. *A man may want to end the damage inflicted by this drug use but not necessarily drug use itself.* Some men may opt for a period of abstinence, without any intention of lifelong abstinence, simply to have time to mend their lives. Others whose lives have become unmanageable will initially set out on a course of lifelong abstinence, sincerely believing that this is the best choice; once their lives have stabilized, though, they begin to consider controlled substance use. Finally, there are men who are unsure about abstinence or controlled use and struggle with ambivalence on a daily basis.

Many who are in recovery, or who are addiction professionals, believe that moderate drug use is not possible once a person has abused drugs. In many cases this is true, but not in all cases. As you will soon see, we have very little understanding of controlled use.

This chapter is neither for nor against controlled use. Whether or not moderate use is indeed viable for former substance abusers remains uncertain. What is certain, however, is that many gay men will aim for controlled use in one form of the other. This chapter helps prepare you for this eventuality.

## CONFLICTING GOALS

Even men whose lives are now utterly out of control and have no doubt that they need to stop using drugs often harbor a secret yet undeveloped plan to resume it once the current turmoil has resolved. I have worked with many men whose lives were devastated by their substance use and who wanted to quit permanently, or in their words, "I don't ever want to go through this again." Still, once the immediate crises passed, their resolution likewise faded. Typically, people who accept that their lives must include ongoing recovery are those who have tried moderate use and failed.

Even if a man recognizes a problem with one drug, he may not have interest in ending all substance use. He may be finished with cocaine or club drugs but still thinks drinking is okay. After all, from his perspective alcohol was never a big issue for him, and he certainly doesn't consider himself an "alcoholic." The same sentiment is often expressed about marijuana: "I'll stop everything but pot." The substance abuser, of course, does not share his plan with his loved ones and helping professionals, knowing full well that this would cause alarm.

What happens if you have different goals for his drug use than he has for himself? You may see that he needs lifelong recovery. He may not be there yet and is instead seeking moderation—the ability to manage his substance use so that it doesn't get out of control. You believe he needs to end all substance use. He admits that certain drugs are dangerous for him, but others are still safe and can be used. You see treatment as a wake-up call to completely reinvent his life. He sees treatment as a respite to put his life back together; he is not looking to make profound structural changes.

## THE LIMITS OF SCIENCE

Many Twelve Step groups and addictions professionals promote the idea that once a person has developed an addiction to a drug, that person can never return to its use. The concept of "powerlessness" supports this belief. Once in recovery, if a man uses his drug of choice, he will inevitably relapse. The recovering addict has full control over the drug as long as it is not in his system; once the drug is inside his body, he cannot fulfill his promises to himself (and others) that "I'll only use this one time." Even years of abstinence from a particular drug does not protect him from his underlying addiction; one use can lead back to complete powerlessness.

Richard Sandor, author of *Thinking Simply about Addiction*, reviewed the available research on recovery and moderate use and decided "Abstinence is necessary for recovery. . . . If you follow true alcoholics for years, you discover those who continue to drink get worse and those who remain abstinent don't. Presumably, the same is true for all other addictions."[1]

Undoubtedly, if a man is abusing drugs or has become dependent (or in less clinical terms, "addicted"), he must stop his use for a time. Continued drug use will only lead to further deterioration. But what happens once his life has stabilized? Is he able to resume any type of substance use, even if this does not include his primary drug or drugs of choice?

Again, you may feel that he needs lifelong abstinence, but this belief may conflict with his own desires and plans. The reality is that in our current understanding of addiction, we can offer only broad-sweeping generalizations on post-treatment options. We don't yet have a completely clear understanding of who can and cannot return to recreational substance use once he or she has experienced abuse or dependence. In one of the most well-received and authoritative books on addiction, *Addiction: From Biology to Drug Policy,* Avram Goldstein, a distinguished addictions researcher, reminds us that, "Some people reject the *controlled-use* approach in principle. . . . In the face of this strong conviction, medical scientists are afraid to even examine the question objectively—a few brave ones did and were pilloried for it. So although experience and common sense warn us that ex-addicts are at exceptionally high risk for relapse, we don't really have scientific proof as to whether controlled use could be realistic for some people in some circumstances, either as an end in itself or as a temporary expedient on the way to total abstinence."[2]

A 2004 conference convened the leading addiction scientists to discuss their research and its implication for treatment.[3] In regard to alcohol use, the conclusion was, "we remain without guidelines concerning who really must stop drinking in order to recover from DSM-IV alcohol dependence, and who can recover stably from dependence even while drinking moderately. While many guidelines exist on *how* to cut down or stop . . . these do not address the question of abstinence versus controlled drinking."[4]

We know even less about other drugs of abuse. For example, does a man need to stop his use of club drugs after recovering from abuse or dependence? There is no clear-cut answer. He may question the need to work toward lifelong abstinence when he sees evidence to the contrary. For example, he can go out to a club and meet men who have been in a rehab and/or outpatient treatment who can now drink sensibly. He can mingle with those who once had the most serious problem with meth or club drugs but who now party without consequence. There is evidence challenging the once unbending and inflexible rule that lifelong abstinence is the only solution. Yet those who study addiction point out that we are only witnessing a snapshot in time of these seeming moderate users. If we watched for several years, we would see a gradual but obvious return to harmful drug use patterns. Questions remain, and in time we will have better guidelines for who can and cannot use moderately once their lives have stabilized. For now, the following recommendations stand:

- Addicts and dependent individuals are less successful at moderate use than substance abusers.

- If a person has tried moderate use in the past without success, the outcome will likely be the same now.

- The method of administration of a drug affects its addictive potential. Smoking a drug or injecting it into a vein leads to an almost immediate impact on the brain, thus increasing its addictive potential. While there are no doubt men out there who have safely managed these forms of administration, I have never worked with one and neither have my peers. Some men were able to use powder cocaine for years without incident, but once it was smoked as crack, their addiction developed quickly. Moderate and safe use of smoked or injected drugs is very difficult.

- Those individuals who began serious drug use at any early age will not likely achieve their goal of moderate use.

- Those who aim for moderate use without making sizable and meaningful changes in their lives will likely have a complete relapse. The epitomes of this are the "dry drunk" and "clean addict" who did indeed stop their substance use but did not otherwise attempt to find avenues of joy, satisfaction, and meaning in their lives. Their lives remain as impoverished mentally, spiritually, and socially as during their addiction.

- Those who have more than one addiction, including gambling, sex, or shopping, are less successful at moderate use.

- Those who have a co-occurring issue such as depression, PTSD, or anxiety are less successful at moderate use.

## AMBIVALENCE

If a man is considering a moderation approach to substance use, you can assume that he is feeling ambivalent about a drug-free lifestyle. Ambivalence is commonly defined as a state of uncertainty when faced with two opposing and/or conflicting desires. It also means holding both positive and negative emotions toward the same person, object, or action. Both definitions are accurate when it comes to continued drug use and ongoing abstinence. There are advantages and drawbacks to each choice, and you can help him weigh each option. By doing so, you are not necessarily promoting controlled use but are instead helping him think realistically through the outcomes of a variety of approaches.

He may choose an abstinence approach when faced with a life that has become totally unmanageable due to his drug use. It's easy for him to convince himself that drug use has no further role in his life when he is on the verge of a jail sentence, when his partner is finally following through on his promise to leave, when there is no money left, or when the latest results show that his T-cells have dropped dramatically. But once these problems fade, so, too, does his promise to himself and to the others in his life. If he stopped drug use simply to please concerned others or has been able to carefully avoid the consequences of substance use—or been repeatedly rescued from these same consequences—his ambivalence about lifelong abstinence lurks close to the surface.

The longer a man's life has revolved around substance use, the more likely he is to experience ambivalence toward quitting. If you ponder this for a few moments, his ambivalence isn't all that mystifying: Drug and alcohol use offer some apparent advantages. For some people, alcohol or other drugs may decrease depression, help with insomnia, relieve pain, alleviate social anxiety, improve sexual performance, or be a source of shared bonding. To genuinely understand a substance abuser's perspective on his use, the disadvantages—although very real and often severe—must be weighed against his perception of the benefits and positive effects of substance use.

According to Carlo DiClemente, one of the pioneers of substance abuse treatment, "There is the very human tendency to generate a pro for every con and a con for every pro. On the one hand, smoking can cause lung cancer; on the other hand, I am young and have a few years before I need to quit. Feeding both sides of the decisional balance scale represents the ambivalence about any kind of change that individuals often experience."[5] When I hear someone say, "I picked up again, but I don't know why," I am sure that underlying ambivalence is one culprit. He will need to give voice to his ambivalence, honor its importance, and decide how to incorporate it into his recovery. Never underestimate the positive side of substance use.

You can help him confront his ambivalence. The most common suggestion for people struggling with ambivalence is to consider all of the *advantages and disadvantages* of substance use. You heard that right: Factor in the advantages of substance use. Collecting evidence against substance use is easy for most people, and most men hope that this acknowledgment will automatically lead to success. It doesn't; instead we must give voice to all of the advantages of substance use. Substance use does offer benefits. If there were absolutely no benefits to his drug use, and he found no pleasure or at least temporary relief from discontent and unhappiness in his drug use, he would have stopped long ago. In a standard intervention, substance users are often asked to answer the following four questions:

1. What are the pros and advantages of continuing your
   substance use?

2. What are the cons and disadvantages of continuing your substance use?

3. What are the pros and advantages of discontinuing your substance use?

4. What are the cons and disadvantages of discontinuing your substance use?

Will, for example, answered these questions with his counselor and came up with these advantages of continued methamphetamine use:

- A decrease in social anxiety (meeting other men at the bars was easier and it made him more assertive in sexual situations).

- It made him feel great.

- Sex was indeed better.

- It helped keep his weight down.

Here are some of the disadvantages he identified for continued meth use:

- The cost.

- Unsafe sex that ALWAYS happened when speeding.

- The emotional and physical crash that occurred after a weekend of party and play.

- A loss of interest in other activities that were once motivating, particularly going to the movies and reading.

Some advantages of stopping meth use were:

- More money in his pocket.

- Less guilt and concern about what he did while bingeing, particularly lingering fears of sexually transmitted diseases.

- Not feeling like crap two to three days each week.

Some disadvantages of stopping meth use were:

- The need to engage in more exercise (possibly even join a gym); this is an activity abhorred by Will.

- He would be more timid about approaching people—this could limit his sexual opportunities.

- Sex would be boring.

- Less energy to complete routine tasks that bore him.

A concerned loved one or helping professional will note that these answers offer insight into other issues that Will needs to address in recovery. Reduced drug use or abstinence may fail if he does not learn assertiveness skills, find ways to maintain his weight, and challenge his beliefs that drug-free sex is boring.

## PERSONAL RESPONSIBILITY

*Once again: An addict may not be 100 percent responsible for an addiction, but he is completely responsible for his recovery.* While the brain is implicated in abuse and addiction, this does not excuse each and every substance abuser and addict from taking responsibility for improving his life. Nobody starts out with a plan to become a drug abuser, or even more serious, an addict. Drug use may make a man less shy about meeting other men, more comfortable taking his clothes off in front of sex partners, decrease his anxiety, or help him feel less ashamed about his sexual identity. For many, drug use just offers pleasure and a method to escape the burdens that pound him each and every day. Many men have no idea how drug use affects their brains, and even fewer know that they have a genetic predisposition for addiction that is in place and ready to be activated once they take their first drink or drug. And even if they are aware of a family predisposition, they are still convinced that it can't happen to them.

Once he does recognize that he has a problem, then he is responsible for his recovery. Even if his brain was preprogrammed in the womb to develop an addiction, this still doesn't absolve him of responsibility for making positive change. Millions of people have made positive changes in their lives after serious drug problems. Each and every person with a substance abuse issue must accept some level of responsibility for the development of this condition, and all are personally and wholeheartedly responsible for their own recovery.

It is certainly easier for a counselor to accept a client's decision to attempt moderation in use than it is for family. Of course some counselors refuse to work with substance abusers until they commit to completely ending their drug use. But what happens when a client doesn't want to end all of his use but rather wants to cut back to less harmful quantities? Do we simply refuse to offer them help? Again, some professionals do, but others are willing to work with them to attempt moderation. I am in the latter group. I will counsel clients for whom moderation may be impossible; for example, a gay man who wants to reduce the amount of methamphetamine he is using is almost always doomed to failure. Still, men want to try.

In the concluding chapter of *Treating Substance Abuse*, a guidebook for practitioners, Edward Rubin, of the Aurora Sinai Medical Center, sums up the experience of many clinicians, including myself: "Some clients are willing to consider the goal of abstinence for themselves, some want to work on moderating their substance use, and yet others want to quit using one drug or another, but continue using something else that they see as nonproblematic. From my perspective, all of these goals may be reasonable and worthy of consideration. From the point of engagement and treatment adherence, it is important to recognize and accept the goals of the individual seeking our services rather than to impose our agenda on him or her. Of course, these original goals may not be our ultimate treatment goals."[6]

Some individuals are successful at moderating their drug use, at least in the short term; it is quite possible that they will slowly return to their damaging patterns over time. Others, though, learn very quickly that moderate use is not possible and that the concept of powerlessness is true, at least for them. At this point, the original goal of moderation now becomes abstinence. But until a client finds success with moderation or has the epiphany of its impossibility, I continue to work with him. Consider the likely outcome if my goal for a client is abstinence but his is moderate use; how long do you think he will continue to seek my services? I would rather be a support in his life than to lose him completely. I often assume a harm-reduction approach in which the decision for or against abstinence is deferred and a slow and deliberate reduction of one's substance use is instead the goal.

But what if you are the loved one of a substance abuser or addict? Allowing him to simply try to use less may be unacceptable to you, particularly if his past use has caused much chaos in his life, and in yours. This is again where the concept of personal responsibility comes into play. You can express strong concern about his decision. But he is the one who must make the decision—he is responsible for his life, and if his choice causes harm to himself and others he cares about, he will need to accept responsibility for the resulting consequences. For loved ones, you need to maintain a tough-love approach and go on with your life; sometimes that means moving on at a distance from the person abusing substances.

I suggest the following steps:

- Thank him for being honest with you. After all, he could have lied and stated he is still practicing abstinence; at least he is up front with you.

- Remind him (and yourself) that the choice is ultimately his.

- Clearly state your displeasure with this decision. Remind him of the numerous problems that substance use caused in his life and the lives of others who love him.

- Offer him education about the difficulties that many men have with moderate use. If he has attempted moderation in the past without success, the odds are definitely against him this time also. Don't lecture. Just offer the facts. Also inform him that what looks like success in the early days to weeks of moderation does not negate what the research says—chances are good that his use can still deteriorate into abuse and addiction.

- Be clear about the consequences. Any consequences that arise from moderate use are his to accept.

- Ask him to discuss his decision with at least three other people, preferably people in recovery. He should weigh the benefits and drawbacks of a return to substance use and discuss his ambivalence. Can he find other ways of meeting the needs that substance use and abuse fulfills for him?

- Refer him to any harm-reduction resources you are aware of. Even if you disagree strongly with his decision, you still don't want him to suffer needlessly. What resources could help minimize any harm that stems from his substance use? I commonly refer patients to tweaker.org for advice on maintaining safety with methamphetamine and club drugs. The resource section at the end of this book offers some suggestions. If he returns to substance use, he can at least learn to minimize the dangers inherent in the act.

- Ask him to write down and share with you the warning signs and indicators that moderate use is escalating into more serious abuse. Phillip, for example, promised his parents that if his drug use caused even one absence from his job, if he engaged in unsafe sexual practices, or if he used more than one to two evenings per week (typically Friday and Saturday), he will seek out help.

- Monitor him. Stand back and await the outcomes. This is all you can do if he opts for moderate use. He might fail, and this failure may occur quickly or slowly. Or, he might succeed or at least maintain moderate use for a long time. Regardless, continue to see him and help him process whatever happens. If he does choose controlled use, he may choose not to see you for some time. Remind him that you are available.

::

Many men whose lives have been wrecked by drug use will still opt for moderate use. Even men who swear never to pick up another drink or drug again—a promise heard often early in treatment—may renege on this oath once life has become stable. While it would, of course, be much safer if he did not choose the very risky option of controlled use, you don't have the final say in the matter. Some men will learn to be moderate users, though most cannot sustain success with this.

Your role is to help him think through the options, and the consequences, considering his past and be willing to help him access treatment if, or when, his experiment fails.

## CHAPTER TEN

# COMMON CHALLENGES FOR GAY MEN IN RECOVERY

THE THREE MOST COMMON CHALLENGES for gay men in recovery are finding new people, places, and things not associated with their former drug use; concerns about HIV and substance use; and how to be sexual without the use of drugs.

Of those three, the most challenging is certainly finding pleasurable and intimately satisfying ways to engage in sexual activity while sober. While actively using, the great majority of gay men used drugs and alcohol to heighten their sexual arousal and extend performance, to hide from their internalized heterosexism, and to increase their comfort in approaching other males for sex. Some men, particularly young men who have been tossed out or have run away from their homes, barter sex for drugs. Even men who have been celibate for years often have sexual underpinnings to their drug use. Gavin, for example, hasn't had any sexual contact with another male for six years, but several times each week he is front of his computer, beer in hand, masturbating to images of naked men on Internet sites.

The Sexuality Information and Education Council of the United States (SIECUS) developed guidelines for comprehensive sexuality education that have become a trusted resource for educators. One of its key concepts is that "sexuality is a central part of being human, and individuals express their sexuality in a variety of ways." Sadly, many adults do not possess even a basic understanding of this key concept, which SIECUS attempts to instill in children in appropriate ways throughout their developmental years. As a foundation for satisfying sexual relationships throughout our lives, SIECUS proposes the following:[1]

- We should take responsibility for our own sexual behavior.

- We should enjoy and express sexuality throughout life.

- We should express our sexuality in ways that are congruent with our values.

- We should discriminate between life-enhancing sexual behaviors and those that are harmful to self and/or others.

- We should be able to express our sexuality while respecting the rights of others.

- We should seek new information to enhance our sexuality.

- We should engage in sexual relationships that are consensual, nonexploitative, honest, pleasurable, and protected.

While this is only one organization's definition of health sexuality, many other organizations that focus on sex education promote the same core elements of a healthy sexual life. Those elements are to enjoy and express our sexuality, consent, nonexploitation, and mutuality, and the need to be cognizant and proactive in seeking new information that can increase sexual satisfaction and growth.

Compare the above guidelines for healthy sexual behaviors to a weekend of meth-induced sexual compulsivity: here safe-sex practices are disregarded, men treat each other as sexual accessories, and the weekend ends with a brain-based dopamine crash on Suicide Tuesday when he wakes up filled with guilt, embarrassment, and maybe even the inability to recall just what he did in the last day or two. How does this compare to the "consensual, nonexploitative, honest, pleasurable, and protected" ideals of SIECUS? While the meth example may seem extreme, many men would opt for the drama and intensity of the drug-fueled episode over the seemingly aseptic SIECUS recommendations.

Some men in recovery may be able to use one or more substances *on occasion* in the future as part of their sexual repertoire. Notice the stress on the words "on occasion." Relying on substance use for sexual activity indicates that either a man's drug problem has not resolved or he is struggling with an underlying issue around his sexual identity that still needs to be addressed, likely internalized heterosexism or shame over sex in general. Others, though, do not have the option of choosing to use occasionally; one episode of drug use is likely to trigger a complete relapse. Regardless of which category he falls into, the ultimate goal is for him to look forward to, and be able to, engage in satisfying sexual activity without the need for chemical enhancement.

## SEXUAL ACTIVITY WITHOUT DRUGS

How, then, does a gay man go about discovering the pleasures of sex without the need for a chemical boost? First, find out where he is at, both physically and psychologically. If you are counseling a newly recovering gay man, it's very likely he is struggling with one or more issues connected with being sexual *without* drugs in the picture. You can help him unearth any problems so the two of you can explore solutions.

Consider exploring some of the following questions:

- Is substance use a means to coping with premature ejaculation, an inability to ejaculate or reach orgasm, and/or pain during sex? (Substance use can temporarily resolve all of the above.)

- Do you see evidence that he has internalized homophobia? This can lead to an inability to feel positive about both oneself and other gay men. Relationships are often unsatisfying, and intimacy is impossible.

- Does he have underlying fears about disease and contamination? With rates of HIV and almost all other sexually transmitted diseases on the rise in the gay community, many men can only overcome their fear of infection via substance use.

- Is he concerned about his body image? Penis size and weight top the list of these concerns in regard to gay male sexual activity. A drug-fueled sexual escapade can ease these worries, at least temporarily.

- Is he concerned about his sexual performance? A man might be so worried about technique or timing of ejaculation that he cannot enjoy sex. His thoughts interfere with satisfaction. Of course, a gay man, similar to any man, might indeed be awkward and clumsy during sexual activity. Despite a widespread belief that gay men are instinctively skilled at sex, this is definitely not the case. There are just as many fumbling and unskilled gay men as straight men. Again, drug use can temporarily lower inhibitions and improve sexual performance (at a long-term price, of course).

- Does he have unrealistic expectations about sexual activity? Too many men imagine sexual activity will resemble scenes and images from adult sexual videos and magazines. In these depictions, sex acts end with a shattering orgasm that leaves both men (and possibly more) shuddering in a pool of sweat-coated sheets. This does happen, but for most men, not consistently. Sexual activity can be fulfilling and pleasurable even without the drama and noise demonstrated in adult male videos. If he expects that this is what sex should be like, he is bound to be disappointed.

All of the above issues can and do interfere with satisfying sex, and using one or more substances can be remove such obstacles, albeit temporarily. Drugs and alcohol are the only conduits many gay men have to otherwise satisfying sex, and many men in early recovery will need support to work on one of more of the above problems. The above list is not comprehensive; other sexual issues may surface that might need intervention, including a history of childhood sexual abuse, or an early teaching that all sex (gay or straight) is dirty or disgusting. Regardless, all are concerns that can lead to unsatisfying sex followed by a relapse to drug use.

Depending on the extent of the damage and risk connected to his current sexual practices, you may suggest he volunteer for a period of sexual abstinence. Some men are relieved to give up this aspect of their lives temporarily, almost as if it were a much-needed vacation. Others rebel against such a suggestion. On the other hand, some men benefit by purposefully engaging in masturbatory fantasies that do not include any images of substance use; many gay male substance abusers have incorporated their drug use even into their sexual fantasies, and refraining from these thoughts is a first step in counter-conditioning the association in their brain between sex and drug use.

For couples struggling with the presence of substance abuse, the sexual concerns of two (or more) partners must now be considered. The obvious question is, how has substance use affected their relationship? Sexologists have learned that sexual dissatisfaction is often an outward sign of numerous relationship issues. Indeed, many couples experience less satisfying sex during periods of drug abuse, which is obvious to both partners, yet they never discuss their feelings. Sexual satisfaction is not likely to increase until the drug abuse is put to an end. When that occurs, these men can then begin to clarify what they do and do not want, and what they like and don't like in regard to sexual activity.

Open communication is the only way we can learn about each other's likes and dislikes, and it's not easy to achieve. The ability to speak openly, without blame or defensiveness, is a learned behavior that is critical for achieving sexual satisfaction. Each partner must be open to hearing what the other has to say, and receptive to feedback without being guarded, critical, retaliatory, and hypersensitive.

Dialogues about sex do not have to be only about dissatisfaction. They can be intimately satisfying discussions that result in mutual discovery as two partners share their fantasies, changing desires, and dreams. Healthy sexual relationships acknowledge that partners change, including sexual desires and motivations. Couples who add variety to their sexual habits— who shake up the routine—revive their passion for each other.

## HIV AND SUBSTANCE USE

As we've discussed, substance use can lead to unsafe sexual practices. Thus an abuser could become infected with HIV or another sexually transmitted disease or possibly even re-infected with a different strain, making medical treatment even more complicated. Gay men who are not infected with HIV may use drugs to temporarily suppress fears of infection while engaging in unsafe sex. And, of course, some substances increase sexual arousal while simultaneously hindering the brain's ability to think logically—a combination that certainly does not encourage safe sex.

What if he is already infected with HIV? Even in this age of antiretroviral drugs to treat HIV—helping those infected live much longer, healthier lives—an HIV-positive diagnosis is terrifying, and many men cope with the terror by simply blotting it out with substance use. This is a form of denial that can work in the short term, but long-term consequences accrue as the virus replicates unimpeded in the body, even though proven medical interventions could help if the abuser would seek care. There is a long list of reasons why substance abuse is even more dangerous for men infected with HIV, and for their partners. Here are a few:

- A drug-abusing lifestyle rarely prioritizes physical health. The more profound the substance use problem, the less likely a man is to be taking care of himself with good nutrition, rest, and exercise, and the less able he is to combat the complications of HIV.

- Some infected men use drugs and alcohol to ease their guilt about possibly passing the virus onto others.

- Some drugs—meth is a prime example—increase the amount of virus in the body.

- Substance abusers are often unable to comply with HIV medication regimens. *Most of us* do not strictly follow the directions for taking medication; substance use only further compounds the problem. For those infected with HIV, just a few missed doses could lead to a failure of the medication, and ominously a whole class of medications. While not every substance user is incapable of adherence to their medication regimen, and I have worked with many a man who did follow them with very few missteps, others— and I fear this is the majority—simply cannot stay on track with their meds.

When gay men are first diagnosed with HIV, they typically turn to friends and romantic partners for support, and families of origin are often purposefully kept in the dark. Yet once they begin to show signs of illness and health complications, they then inform their families of origin. Siblings are typically told first, then the mother, followed last by the father. I have seen a diagnosis bring families closer together, but so, too, have I seen it further divide them. I have also seen it annihilate long-standing romantic relationships, particularly when one man is HIV positive and the other is not. Common reactions by family members and loved ones include guilt, stress, rejection, anxieties about death, hopelessness, rage, blaming the gay man, infantilizing behavior, and even fears of contamination.

If you are caring for such a man—either as a helping professional or as a caring other—keep this in mind. He is now struggling with at least three stigmas: (1) he is a gay male; (2) he is HIV positive; and (3) he is a substance abuser. His HIV disclosure may open the door to family secrets left unexplored for decades—this can be a highly stressful time for everyone.

Family members and other caring friends can help their loved one by first educating themselves on HIV and its treatment. Next, it's important that they establish their own support system to deal with their emotions regarding the diagnosis. They can also help their loved one comply with his medication regimen and can support him in ending or markedly decreasing his drug use. Finally, friends and loved ones can work on repairing the rifts that may have created distance in their relationship with the gay man, particularly those arising from his sexuality.

Here are some essential actions he will need to take to maintain his health:

- *Follow the treatment protocol.* Whatever treatment his physicians recommend, he needs to comply with it. Even though his doctor likely specializes in treating infectious diseases, he still needs to be actively involved in his own care, rather than a passive receptacle for his doctor's recommendations. There are numerous HIV information web sites and social service agencies that can help him gain the knowledge and skills to collaborate on his treatment.

- *Disclose current and past substance use and abuse.* It is critical that he tell his doctor that he is using or abusing drugs and/or alcohol; their use can affect treatment compliance and way his body metabolizes medications. Also, there are adverse interactions between some medications for HIV and those for addiction.

- *Disclose any mental health conditions.* The need for disclosure also holds true for mental health conditions, including depression, bipolar disorder, obsessive compulsive disorder, and any mental health condition he takes medication for. The combination of substance abuse and a psychiatric condition complicates treatment for HIV. If he cannot follow a medication regimen right now, he and his doctor will need to develop a new plan of action. His treatment

team may advise him to begin substance abuse treatment, possibly
even enter a rehab, and regain stability in his life before starting
medication for HIV. The more unmanageable his life has become,
the less likely he will take his HIV medications correctly.

- *Cope with the psychological impact of HIV.* There is a stunning
  dichotomy between the generation that survived the early decades
  of HIV (a generation that watched the decimation of their breth-
  ren) and the one that followed. The former still sees the disease as
  a death sentence. The latter has less fear since they have been told
  repeatedly that HIV is a chronic condition. For that reason, unsafe sex is again on the rise for younger men, much of it fueled by
  the use of drugs and alcohol. While a diagnosis of HIV no longer
  means death, it doesn't mean one can go about his life as if nothing has changed. Each person infected with HIV will have his own
  reaction to the diagnosis: terror, apathy, anger, relief (for those
  who believed that contracting the condition was inevitable), rage,
  depression, guilt, self-blame. Likewise, each person will have to
  process his own idiosyncratic reactions and plan for a future as an
  HIV-positive person. This is where professional counseling is especially valuable, particularly when family members are not comfortable discussing this topic or the topic of sexuality, or are dealing
  with their own stunned reaction to the diagnosis.

- *Acknowledge that one drug can lead to the use of another.* Sub-
  stituting one drug for another is rarely successful. For example, he
  might suggest giving up his meth while continuing the "safe" activity of drinking alcohol. However, after a few drinks, his resolve to
  stay away from meth quickly fades. Indeed, using one substance
  often triggers the use of others, even those he is committed to abstaining from. If he finds that such substitutions are not working,
  this needs to be explored with his counselor; maybe he will need to
  consider lifelong abstinence.

- *Gather current knowledge about safe sex.* In my work with teen-
  agers, some of the most ridiculous misinformation regarding safe
  sexual practices is accepted at face value. Being able to offer accurate information or even a resource for this information is indeed
  valuable.

- *Understand the connection between sexual activity and drug use.* Remember that sexual thoughts and feelings can quickly lead to cravings and urges for drug use. The brain has formed a conditioned association between the two. Breaking the connection entails undergoing periods of sexual abstinence, modifying sexual fantasies, and engaging in satisfying sexual activity without the use of drugs or alcohol. Eventually, the brain will stop automatically desiring drug use whenever sexual arousal occurs.

- *Work with a professional to increase sober sexual satisfaction.* He will need help conceptualizing a plan for the future that addresses all of the physical, psychological, and relationship issues that can lead to unsafe sex. And he will need help finding satisfaction with safe sex. Getting this support will greatly increase his chances of success.

If he is newly seeking support for his drug use, he may be unsure of his HIV status and afraid to find out, since he probably engaged in high-risk drug use and/or sexual activity. If so, urge him to get tested. Some gay men test several times each year, while others have never been tested. For a man who has engaged in unsafe practices, the thought of the test is a specter hanging over his life. He already knows he should take the test, but his fears of testing positive are overpowering and prevent him from taking action. He fears the results, their impact on his life, and how others will respond. Far too many gay men have hesitatingly informed their families that they were HIV positive only to be met with stony silence or reprimands of "I told you so." Such disclosure is even more difficult if he and the family have never discussed his sexuality. He'll need support before and after the test, even if the results are negative.

## PEOPLE, PLACES, AND THINGS REVISITED

According to the U.S. Department of Health and Human Services, "The number of gay coffee shops, bookstores, and activities that do not involve alcohol and drugs is increasing, but gay bars and parties that focus on alcohol and drug use are by far the best advertised and most identifiable elements of gay social life."[2]

Indeed, bars and clubs are the assumed birthright of many a gay man. Even in the most rural of areas, there always seems to be a nearby hangout for the GLBT crowd. Large urban areas have their "gay ghettos," neighborhoods where gay men and gay businesses abound; and of course these neighborhoods have at least one bar, and often far more than that. But whether in a large urban gay ghetto or a nondescript small-town bar, wherever gay men choose to congregate there is also the likelihood of alcohol and drug use. Since substance use is so common in the gay male community, it is often assumed to be normal; those who don't use alcohol or drugs seem to be the odd ones or are presumed to be in recovery.

One of the most challenging tasks for a gay man in recovery will be to change his social life, particularly his recreational and social habits. While this is true for anyone working toward recovery, it is more concerning for gay men, since bars and clubs are an integral part of many of their lives. To simply tell them that they need to change this lifestyle will not go over well, or, in the words of Dana Finnegan and Emily McNally in their book *Counseling Lesbian, Gay, Bisexual, and Transgender Substance Abusers:*

> LGBT bars and clubs are much more than bars or clubs; oftentimes they
> are the one place where lesbian, gay, bisexual, or transgendered people
> can go and be reasonably sure that most of the others in that bar are
> like them. . . . Traditionally, then, LGBT bars and clubs have been the
> places where people could go and feel relatively safe in making social
> and/or sexual overtures to others of the same sex and/or gender iden-
> tity. These bars and clubs have also traditionally been the places where
> people would go and make contact—they were the places to meet others
> like themselves. Thus it does not work to flatly state, "Look, if you don't
> want to get hit by the train, don't sit on the tracks. So don't go to bars/
> clubs." For many LGBTs, that is like telling them that their social life is
> over—that they can no longer go to what is often the only place avail-
> able to meet other LGBTs in a relatively safe atmosphere.[3]

Of course, not every gay man chooses to socialize in bars and clubs, and for others attendance is sporadic to rare. Some men sit at home drinking themselves into oblivion while using the services of Internet porn, a rented "escort," or a new friend met on Craig's List, while others are at bathhouses and private gyms ingesting one or more substances for a night of sexual excitement. And, of course, there are circuit parties. In every case, we are asking gay men to give up not only drug use but the sexual activities and high-risk environments he enjoys, especially bars and clubs. How then can we be stunned when they begin drug use again?

Rather than staying away from these common social outlets completely, help him look for alternative and safer ways to socialize. Here are some suggestions:

- Temporarily abstain from bars and clubs for several months until his life has become more manageable.

- Seek out members of the gay community who are recovering. There are sober recovery groups for gay men and women, and some of these include opportunities for socializing in settings that discourage drug use.

- Attend a Twelve Step meeting before going to one of the above high-risk environments.

- Go to bars or clubs with a sober group of friends.

There is no surefire solution for this common concern, and the above suggestions may not work for him. But some men do make this work, and if these settings are that important to your loved one, it is worth trying. Straight men and women have a variety of "clean and sober" social outlets that confirm their identity while they are in recovery. Sexual minorities, in contrast, do not.

::

Chances are that your loved one will be coping with at least one of the common challenges described in this chapter; some men will be struggling with two and even all three. Of course, this is in addition to the other recovery issues and obstacles that every person encounters regardless of sexual orientation. He can manage all of this with understanding, support, and professional involvement. With support, he can rebuild or possibly create for the very first time a satisfying life as a gay male.

## CHAPTER ELEVEN

# PARTNER RELATIONSHIPS

*By the very nature of marriage vows, to love, honor, and cherish, honesty is an important ingredient. Within Western society, marriage is usually viewed as being based on love and full partnership. Yet, addiction is built upon secrets and lies.*

—Erica Orloff, in *Can Marriage Survive Addiction?*

LET'S MAKE THIS POINT ABSOLUTELY CLEAR at the very beginning of this chapter: Substance abuse is by far a greater deal breaker in gay male relationships compared with straight and lesbian couples. As you will learn in this chapter, gay men will end their relationship over a substance use problem far quicker than straight men and women of all sexual orientations.

Just as we are liberal in the definition of "family," our definition of "relationship" for gay men is equally expansive. For example, a gay man may be involved in romantic relationships that involve three or more romantically entwined individuals. What happens if Adam, Bob, Charles, and Daniel share the same house, each other's beds, and each other's passions, but Bob has a substance abuse problem? All are undoubtedly affected in one form or another, but how do they get the help they need? Couples therapy for substance abuse has traditionally focused on the couple as we commonly understand the word—that is, consisting of two people. However, polls and surveys find that gay men are most inventive in fashioning relationships that meet their myriad needs, and these relationships often contain more than a duo. That said, so as not confuse readers (and myself as I write this chapter), I will assume that most readers are involved in a more traditional construction of a romantic couple. If this model does not fit your own current relationship, tailor the information to suit your needs.

## FOR PARTNERS

If you are in a romantic relationship, "union," or marriage (in those states or countries that permit such a commitment), this chapter is meant to be shared. Both you and your partner should acknowledge how substance use has affected your relationship and be alert to the challenges that await you in the recovery process. If one man in a relationship has a substance abuse or dependence problem, it always affects the other involved male. Robert Ackerman, cofounder of the National Association for Children of Alcoholics, said that addiction "is not a spectator sport." By that, he meant you cannot stand outside of the suffering your loved one is experiencing.

Earlier in this book I said that the first step for any substance abuser is to stop using all substances for at least three months. It takes at least this long for the brain to sufficiently repair itself. You, as the non-abusing partner, will also have to change your behavior during his early recovery. Stop or refrain, in your loved one's presence, from all recreational drug use so you don't tempt him needlessly. This includes alcohol and tobacco. This move might include adjusting your social life during this time period, as bars and clubs are a risk factor. Stay calm as you read this request. I am not asking you to swear off recreational substance use for a lifetime, and you can certainly start again in the near future. But for your partner's sake and the sake of your relationship, I'm asking you to remove all temptations for the time being. If your loved one has a problem with prescription medications but you need them for your own medical condition (narcotic painkillers are an example), please put them in a spot that he cannot access or locate. And refrain from being "under the influence" in his presence; this, too, is a temptation and your impaired judgment may lead you to give in to his pleading, or any of his other suggestions for how to approach recovery without remaining abstinent.

What if both men in the relationship have a substance abuse or addiction problem? This predicament is certainly problematic and weighted toward failure. I promise you that one partner cannot continue on with his drug use while the other makes a sincere effort at recovery. Failure is inevitable. This is true even if you have different drugs of choice; for example, if he likes meth while you opt for alcohol, this failed outcome will not differ. Either both begin the recovery process or look at ending the relationship. I know that this sounds harsh, and that is deliberate. Either you will lead him back to substance use or he will do the same to you. How does an alcoholic stay clean when his lover has a fully stocked bar at home? How does a man refrain from methamphetamine use when his boyfriend is into the drug and the sexual activity it fosters? These relationships simply won't work for men in recovery, but that doesn't stop countless gay men from trying. I have repeatedly witnessed gay men enter rehab with the full intent of achieving abstinence and resurrecting their lives, yet refuse to touch the issue of their partner's substance abuse. And in spite of the fantastic progress they make in this setting, they will inevitably revert to substance abuse within days of returning home. So let me repeat: Two substance-abusing individuals in a relationship in which one refuses to change will lead to failure.

Even if both men commit to abstain from or reduce their substance use, there is still no guarantee that the relationship will survive. Erase any romantic notion you might have of the two of you struggling together to overcome addiction. The misty image of both of you side by side warding off the perniciousness of substance use may make good fodder for the theater, a film, a song, or at the least a cable movie of the week, but it doesn't often lead to mutual success. Your recovery needs will be different than his. Some challenges you will be unable to help him with, and vice versa. Your temptations will not necessarily be his. What if he fails while you maintain abstinence? Seemingly, you could help him regain his traction, but in reality the outcome is likely to be different: he instead pulls you back into the lifestyle you so desperately wanted to escape. With sufficient commitment and motivation, it's true that you can both resolve an addiction problem and restore the integrity of your relationship, but depending just how large a role substance abuse played in your relationship, you may eventually recognize you share very little other than substance use.

## THE CHALLENGES OF GAY MALE RELATIONSHIPS

Intimate relationships bring life's greatest joys, yet they are also the source of our greatest irritations, stressors, and pains. The romantic relationships of gay men are complicated by numerous issues and challenges that het-erosexual couples do not confront. While there are problems that all couples face, regardless of sexual orientation (such as boredom, waning sexual interest, communication, and financial differences), some prob-lems are indeed specific to gay male couples—and these problems can make or break their partnership. When we then factor in substance abuse or dependence on the part of one or both men, we find that their relation-ship is very tenuous and fragile. Substance use and dependence damages relationships and affects trust, finances, the choice of friends and social outlets, and even the insight to notice the warning signs that two men are hurting one another.

Let's briefly look at the most common forces that destroy same-sex relationships. We will then layer another level of complexity through the addition of substance abuse.

## Internalized Homophobia

A gay man who has internalized negative messages about homosexual-ity tends to believe on some level that he is somehow inadequate or dam-aged. He often feels shame about his identity, does not trust other people, and stays emotionally distant in relationships. Obviously, these are not ideal characteristics for a healthy long-term relationship.

It is difficult for another person to love us if we don't love ourselves (unless, of course, we find another gay man who is equally internally ho-mophobic and this really sets up some harmful relationship dynamics). If a gay man feels ashamed about his sexual identity, he will probably not be comfortable showing physical contact in public places, he will have difficulty with intimacy, and the issue of trust will surface repeatedly.

## Gender-Role Conflict

Men are taught to be independent, self-reliant, powerful, aggressive, com-petitive; to hide any sign of weakness (particularly emotions such as fear and sadness); and to undervalue empathy skills. They are certainly not taught how to take the perspective of another person. When two men in a relationship share the same gender roles, they often encounter an outright war; simple chores such as cooking dinner, cleaning dishes, and paying bills are perilously fraught with unintentional discord. In sum, many men do not know how to seek emotional support and nurturance from another man or how to give it when their partner is in need of just such treatment.

## Lack of Support

Another relationship difficulty is the lack of social support for gay relationships. The most obvious is that the legal world has by and large prevented many gay men and women from receiving benefits taken for granted by heterosexual couples—including tax breaks, insurance benefits, and control of medical decisions in catastrophic incidents.

Societal disapproval of gay relationships also presents problems that one might not immediately consider in comparison to the high-profile challenges just mentioned. At the top of the list is family members who are less than enthusiastic about or even outright unwilling to acknowledge a son's or brother's sexuality, and, to add insult to injury, the existence of his male partner. Gay men who have been together for years may have to hide their relationship in order not to disturb one or more family members. Additionally, although most straight couples have extended families they can turn to when problems arise in life, this cannot be assumed for a male couple. Their families may not be accepting of a gay relationship or are simply uncomfortable with the concept of two men in a loving relationship. As a result, a troubled gay man may not feel comfortable turning to his family when a relationship begins to go astray, as he knows they will not offer him support.

## Brief Courtship

It never ceases to amaze me that so many gay men jump right through the courtship stage and begin a serious relationship—often moving in together—after only several months. Gay relationship expert Betty Berzon wrote that if she had her way, gay couples would have to wait at least six months before they moved in together. During this time they would have to actually get to know each other as whole people, not just as sexual beings.

Coming to fully know another person is a process that takes years, even decades. And even then, we always have secrets that those we love aren't privy to. We certainly cannot truly know another person's foibles, emotional baggage, and unpleasant habits in a few short months, particularly when both partners are attempting to make the very best impression on each other. However, many gay men either don't know this, as they had limited dating experience in adolescence, or simply don't care while in the throes of passion. But after a year, the real challenges of the relationship begin, and many will find themselves living with another man they are incompatible with, or, worse, don't even like.

## The Easy Termination of Gay Relationships

One of the advantages of a publicly recognized and socially sanctioned union such as marriage is that it discourages people from simply ending a relationship when problems arise; it is more difficult for one or both partners to just walk away without any lasting consequence. Most gay men, on the other hand, expect a quick and comparatively painless dissolution to their relationship when problems and challenges become evident. The ability to easily end a relationship when the blissful stage is punctured by the reality that comes with two people mapping a life together reduces the chance that two men will hang in there and work out problems.

## Monogamy

Monogamy ranks as one of the most contentious issues for gay male couples. Read my book *Boy Crazy* if you are interested in more information on this fascinating topic. Feeling sexual desire for another person outside of an established romantic relationship is part of the human condition. Not surprisingly, many people fail at monogamy, regardless of their sexual orientation. But it is gay men who are most challenged by monogamy. If research accurately reflects the reality of gay male relationships, all too many gay men engage in sexual activity with another person outside of their relationship and much of this activity remains a secret. As for strict long-term monogamy in which we have absolutely no involvement with another sexual partner other than the man already in our lives—well, that level of monogamy is unusual in gay male relationships. Indeed, this is one of the main reasons established gay couples enter therapy: They want to explore the option of an "open relationship." (Typically however, one member is far more enthusiastic about this freedom than the other.)

For gay couples that are not interested in monogamy and instead want some version of an "open relationship," sexual activity with another person (or persons) outside of the primary relationship will not be a tumultuous issue. However, a trend that I and other professionals who work in the areas of human sexuality and couples counseling have noted in the past several years is a resurgence of a desire, by gay men, for monogamous relationships.

Look at the many challenges gay male relationships face: internalized heterosexism, a lack of societal support, gender-role conflict, a too-brief courtship period before moving in together and swearing commitment for life, monogamy, and the ease of ending relationships. Isn't it easy to understand just how difficult a gay male relationship can be? Let's also acknowledge that young gay men do not have role models in the gay male community for long-term relationships that endure the ups and downs of life. The couples that have managed this feat remain hidden from our day-to-day lives. When we also consider that many gay men, due to delayed adolescence, are not blossoming sexually until their thirties, forties, and fifties and are only then engaging in romantic and sexual adventures that straight men typically completed in their teens and early twenties, the complexities of gay relationships are mind-boggling. And now, as if not already complex enough, we will factor in substance abuse and addiction.

## SUBSTANCE ABUSE AND ROMANTIC RELATIONSHIPS

When a romantic partner initially recognizes that his partner has a substance abuse problem, he tries to help as much as possible. And just as often, the problem gets worse instead of better while the non-abusing spouse feels increasing resentment, frustration, and hopelessness. This is a no-win situation for all involved. Consider some of the challenges that non-abusing partners face; if you are that person, most likely some but not all of these challenges occurred in your relationship.

If you are the partner who does not abuse substances, you may have initially been suspicious of how much your partner was really using drugs. If you at first held back from directly confronting him or only hesitatingly expressed your concerns, this is normal. However, as the severity of substance use became more noticeable and unavoidable, your initial whispers of concerns grew into cajoling, pleading, and even attempts at humiliating him into quitting or at least cutting back on his drug use. You may have tried logic to get him to see the looming consequences of his actions. You may well have also lost your temper and threatened consequences. Your partner responded by making halfhearted attempts at stopping or cutting back, becoming better at hiding his use, or claiming that others were wildly exaggerating his substance use.

As problems such as these escalate, the probability of the relationship ending suddenly increases. Within straight marriages, most women

## WHAT CHALLENGES DO YOU RECOGNIZE?

• Are you building a growing number of resentments? Are you stressed, angry, and depressed?

• Are you hypervigilant, always searching for warning signs that substance use and its consequences are about to pounce? Do you live with chronic anxiety? Are you always on edge, not knowing when the next binge is going to occur or always waiting for the "other shoe to drop"?

• Do you doubt your own sanity? Substance abusers and addicts often lie and manipulate in order to get their way, and living with a person skilled in such manipulation can make one doubt one's own judgment of what is real. Promises to stop always seem to be broken, often sooner than later.

• Do you have to hide money and valuables?

• Has your social life taken a direct hit? As your partner's recreational use progresses into substance abuse and addiction, is your range of friends and social outlets dwindling? Do you isolate yourself from friends and family to keep up a facade of normalcy?

• Have you been abused, either physically or verbally? This can include while your partner was under the influence of one or more substances or at any time. The same statistics that apply to straight couples apply to gay couples: The majority of physical abuse takes place when drug and/or alcohol use is occurring.

will remain with a husband long after he develops a substance use problem, even if this problem is severe. The opposite most certainly does not hold true: The majority of men will leave their wife if she develops a substance abuse problem. We can glean from this that men in general will not stick it out when addiction occurs in their marriage or relationship. But when you consider all of the abovementioned challenges inherent in gay male relationships, it is no wonder that so many end when a substance use problem complicates shared lives.

If you don't leave, you begin to shoulder more and more responsibility for the relationship. The amount you take on is in direct proportion to the amount the substance abuser cedes. Eventually, you reach a state of homeostasis, no matter how unhealthy this tenuous stability may be. When sharing your life with a drug abuser, it is nearly impossible to avoid creating—at least in the short term—patterns that allow him to continue using without experiencing the full force of its repercussions. Especially in the beginning of a problem, we will try to create a semblance of normalcy and manageability, one that often permits his substance use to further spiral out of control. You would think that we gay men, as vanguards of new relationship models in which honesty about thorny sexual activities abound, would necessarily be more frank and candid in all of our interactions. After all, if we can openly discuss threesomes, fuck buddies, open relationships, and desires for non-monogamy with our partners, it shouldn't be so difficult to approach the topic of substance use in this very same relationship. However, this theory is wrong. If the non-abusing partner remains in a relationship with the drug user (and this is doubtful), the couple tends to develop the same destructive practices that mark all couples coping with substance abuse and addiction. As for those couples with multiple partners, we simply don't have an understanding yet of the complexity of this issue.

So let's summarize: If you are a couple in which one person has some form of substance use problem, the most likely outcome is that your relationship will end. If your relationship doesn't end and substance use continues (and even escalates), it will inevitably erode into a pattern that is typical of most such relationships, one that drains the life and love from your partnership.

## AL-ANON

Because so many in the treatment field are in recovery themselves, they tend to promote the same tools and interventions that they used for their recovery. If it worked for me, their thinking goes, it will work for everybody. And when it comes to couples coping with addiction, the standard recommendation is Al-Anon. For those unfamiliar with this type of self-help group, Al-Anon helps spouses and other family members detach from shame and guilt associated with their loved one's alcohol or drug use, and also offers support for stopping attempts to control their loved one's use. In effect, the goal is to recognize one's powerlessness over another adult's behaviors. These meetings *never* imply that the non-using partner is responsible for the addict's drug use. However, the same challenges that confront gay men attempting to find a safe Twelve Step meeting also exist for their partners when they are seeking an Al-Anon or other support group. Overall, most partners of gay male substance abusers do not attend these meetings.

## BEHAVIORAL COUPLES THERAPY

The National Registry of Evidence-Based Programs and Practices, an effort by the national Substance Abuse and Mental Health Services Administration,[1] lists behavioral couples therapy as an effective evidence-based treatment for addiction that supports a drug- and alcohol-free lifestyle and enhances your relationship.

William Fals-Stewart and Timothy J. O'Farrell, pioneers in treating addiction as a couples issue, developed behavioral couples therapy.[2] Their research finds that couples often have better outcomes—such as longer abstinence and improved relationships—when they make a collaborative effort to put the substance-abusing member of the couple on a path to recovery. In their model, substance abuse leads to a vicious cycle for couples. As drug use escalates, negative feelings, withdrawal, and relationship dissatisfaction occur for both men. This in turn leads to even more substance abuse. Behavioral couples therapy intervenes in all of these unhelpful relationship behaviors and patterns by guiding couples toward behavior changes that will benefit their relationship; changes in feelings soon follow. The authors state that abstinence is absolutely necessary if you want to see lasting change in your relationship.

Look at the expectations and assignments in the next several pages, and see if you are willing to try behavioral couples therapy with guidance from a counselor or therapist.

## The Four Promises

Behavioral couples therapy has four promises at its foundation. To follow behavioral couples therapy, both you and your partner must agree to abide by the following promises for the next three months:

1. You will not threaten to end the relationship. This does not mean you are signing up for a lifetime commitment, simply that over the next three months neither of you will threaten to end the relationship. One or both of you may still be considering this option, but for the next three months, don't speak on the topic, and, if possible, don't dwell on it in your own minds. You can't even use the threat as retaliation or in anger.

2. You will not be violent or threaten violence. This is particularly relevant if you have ever had any violence in your relationship. For the next three months you will not threaten violence or use any equally intimidating behavior.

3. You will both focus on the present and the future rather than the past. It is all too easy to stay focused on the wrongs of the past, particularly when you have built up a wall of resentment. But for the next three months, you're not going to fling past faults and misbehaviors in each other's faces no matter how tempting it may be, or how angry you are. Experience shows that it is usually the non-drug-using man who is more challenged by this promise.

4. You will both commit mutually to change. Working as a couple on ending your substance use and improving your relationship is an active process, not one that you can do passively from your chair. It requires work, and like all meaningful activities, the more effort you put into it, the more successful you will be.

## Daily Trust Discussion

Behavioral couples therapy adds a new ritual into your life: the daily trust discussion. Together you decide on a block of time, of at least several minutes, that you can spend together every day; the best time for this routine is typically the morning, but couples are free to choose whatever time best suits both of them. During these few minutes, you will face each other and complete the following ritual:

- The substance-using man states his intention to stay abstinent that day and thanks his spouse for his support.

- His partner thanks him for his efforts at abstinence.

In the following example, Peter, the substance user of the couple, turns to his partner, Kareem, and initiates the daily routine:

Peter: "I have been drug and alcohol free for the last twenty-four hours and plan to remain drug and alcohol free for the next twenty-four hours. Thank you for listening and being supportive of my effort to be abstinent."

Kareem: "Thank you for staying drug and alcohol free for the last twenty-four hours. I appreciate the effort you are making to stay clean and sober."

Remember, this is only an example; the script you devise with your partner will certainly bear the imprint of your own relationship. Notice, though, that there is no bitter arguing, debate, threats, sarcasm, anger-fueled rants about past failures, or subtle (or even not-so-subtle) questioning of each other's sincerity and the future of the relationship.

All the exchange consists of is a simple promise to try to remain abstinent for the next day and mutual thanks for each other's efforts. It sounds so easy, but it can be immeasurably challenging to carry out. Many couples roll their eyes when introduced to this exercise, particularly when they are both feeling angry and resentful. Consider this a minor barrier.

If both of you commit to a three-month effort at improving your relationship, you will have a good chance of success if you focus on the four promises that are the foundation for this improvement. Pay particular attention to the fourth promise: you will both actively participate in this effort.

## Catch Your Partner Doing Something Nice

Behavioral couples therapy uses several activities to increase positive feelings and commitment in a relationship. Often couples affected by substance abuse are sorely lacking in these qualities. In this activity, both you and your partner acknowledge one nice thing you have done for each other during the last twenty-four hours. These do not have to be dramatic displays of goodwill; even those small, seemingly mundane activities that occur in a shared life will do. Behaviors such as making the bed, straightening the house, letting you sleep in, paying a bill, and complimenting you on your appearance all count. Most often, couples affected by substance abuse no longer acknowledge these small details; instead their interactions are often arguments or efforts to minimize contact as soon as possible, each man withdrawing into his own private world.

## Shared Activities

In *Behavioral Couples Therapy for Alcoholism and Drug Abuse,* Timothy O'Farrell and William Fals-Stewart explain that couples "may not enjoy each other's company anymore. Hobbies, sports, and other interests often take a back seat to trying to keep the family together, the bills paid, and the substance abuser out of trouble."[3]

Shared activities are another proactive attempt to foster positive feelings in your relationship. Many couples coping with substance abuse no longer share any activities together, even those they once enjoyed. Spending time doing fun activities together will work to bring the couple closer. These activities can be enjoyed with or without the company of additional people; it all depends on the desires of each partner. Of course, all activities should be supportive of abstinence, so a jaunt to the local gay nightclub is not an option. Try for one mutually planned and shared activity a week.

## Caring Day

A caring day is a day that one of you plans ahead of time and that includes several activities that you know will please your partner. These do not have to be elaborate or expensive endeavors. For example, my partner knows that a caring day for me would include dinner out and a film at our local art cinema, but for him it would be an afternoon at Sam's Club followed by a meal. The partner organizing the caring day should rotate weekly.

## Communication Skills and Problem-Solving Training

Couples coping with substance abuse often feel bitter and hostile, and their communication tends to be minimal and inadequate. Behavioral couples therapy teaches a couple to practice good communication, listening skills, and problem solving and resolution.

Here are some principles of effective communication:

- using "I" statements

- expressing negative feelings with words instead of actions

- being assertive, not aggressive

- monitoring your nonverbal communication (that is, voice volume, posture, gestures, and eye contact)

- avoiding behaviors such as accusations, sulking, withdrawing, and violence

Good communication skills require the ability to listen as well as speak. Successful listening includes the following:

- giving your full attention

- acknowledging what the other person is saying

- keeping your own talk to a minimum

- listening with empathy

- actively solving problems together, not making unilateral decisions

∷

At some point, the romantic partners of a substance abuser recognize that they are involved in a threesome: two men *and* drugs/and or alcohol. As a romantic partner, you will soon recognize that the man you share your life with is intimately invested in his drug or drugs of choice. Your real-life relationship is now secondary to his relationship with his substance use and abuse. When behavioral couples therapy is joined to the core components of recovery—abstinence and changes in thinking, behaving, and feeling—you have established a foundation for success. When concerned others lend support to your efforts, you are even more likely to have positive outcomes.

## CHAPTER TWELVE

::

# FOR ALL LOVED ONES: THE MEANING OF LIFE (WITHOUT DRUGS)

AS YOUR LOVED ONE PROGRESSES in a life not reliant on substance use, he will be tackling other problems, one by one. Some are practical, such as money management skills, anger management, and continued work on relationships. Others are of a philosophical and existential nature, the most pressing being the meaning and purpose of his life. Not exploring this question risks a life built on fragile foundations, a life that can lead back to problematic drug use. It may take a long time before he can address this question, but address it he must at some point for continued success with his substance use goals and, of even greater value, a satisfying life.

## COMPOUNDED LOSSES

Thus far the process of abstinence has required that your loved one give up many of the most enjoyable and satisfying activities in his life. No doubt using drugs led to negatives consequences for him, but even so, he certainly felt pleasure. To achieve abstinence, he has sworn off drugs and alcohol, the company of high-risk people in his life, places he frequented (such as bars and clubs), and possibly even sexual activity he was accustomed to, and still desires.

Abstinence is a process of compounded losses, and your loved one cannot help but experience abstinence—at least in the beginning—as a process of excising myriad parts of his life and identity, some of which he holds very dear. And though you can stand there on the sidelines cheering him on and offering him visions of the wondrous substance-free life that is possible for him, he will still feel these losses. In early recovery he will feel grief, doubt, disillusionment, and misgivings about his choice of abstinence. A patient once told me that even the worst day he had since beginning a drug-free lifestyle ten years ago doesn't compare to the very best day of his drug use. During early recovery such a mind-set is impossible for many gay men to adopt. Instead, many feel their lives are over; all of the excitement, joy, and intensity have been banished. Clearly, such a mind-set does not bode well for a continued drug-free lifestyle.

In the wise words of Dr. Richard Sandor, author of *Thinking Simply about Addiction,* "Abstinence, though necessary, is simply self-denial. Recovery, on the other hand, is the affirmation of a life wisdom that brings the abstinent alcoholic or addict to a place where he no longer wants to be intoxicated, no matter what life throws at him."[1]

Abstinence necessitates loss, while recovery requires building a new life. How can your loved one move past self-denial and reach the point where he no longer wants to go through the days and years under the influence of one or more substances? Granted, it's a gigantic leap, but an untold number of people have traversed this chasm. Sadly, though, some people may successfully stop drug use but never make any otherwise meaningful change in their lives. They never fashion a new reality or new identity and thus end up miserable creatures that inflict bitter emotional pain on themselves and their families. You might have heard of these people referred to "dry drunks" and "clean addicts." Not filling up the yawning gaps in one's life that come from relinquishing the fleeting joys of substance use (the more serious the drug use, the greater the gaps) leads to either relapse or an empty and dissatisfying existence. Sandor describes these people as follows: "The alcoholic may be 'dry,' the addict 'clean,' without recovery, but there is no restoration of a fully human life with its successes and failures, joys and sorrows, acceptance and forgiveness. Instead, there is the gray rigidity of a life lived by the 'safety first' policy, a sense that the addict has put himself in a behavioral box with little room for all the risks inherent in a life fully lived." Sandor refers to the abstinence of a dry drunk or clean addict as a "brittle achievement."[2]

How, then, does your loved one restructure a new life built of stable bricks instead of sticks and hay, one that offers ample opportunities for drug-free sources of joy and that will not topple over at the slightest evidence of life's inevitable tumult? All people in recovery face this challenge and use many of the same approaches. Still, there are a few that are most applicable to gay men.

## A MEANINGFUL LIFE

In the journal *American Psychologist,* Martin Seligman and Mihaly Csikszentmihalyi explore the question of what makes a life meaningful from the perspective of psychology:

> [P]sychologists have scant knowledge of what makes life worth living. They have come to understand quite a bit about how people survive and endure under conditions of adversity. However, psychologists know very little about how normal people flourish under more benign conditions. Psychology has, since World War II, become a science largely about healing. It concentrates on repairing damage within a disease model of human functioning. This almost exclusive attention to pathology neglects the fulfilled individual. . . .[3]

Almost all addiction research focuses on methods, interventions, and techniques to end substance use and maintain this abstinence. But while ending or cutting back on substance use is necessary, is it alone sufficient for a satisfying and meaningful life? Compare the two following quotes:

> Psychological well-being cannot be simply the absence of distress and conflict, any more than physical health is the absence of disease.
> —Christopher Peterson, in *American Psychologist*[4]

> [R]ecovery from addiction is not merely the absence of the disease of addiction. Recovery is the development of an entirely new and a far better life. In other words, recovery is not about restoring addicts to where they were before their drug and alcohol use.
> —Robert L. DuPont interview, in *Counselor*[5]

Indeed, both physical and mental health are more than the absence of disease. Recovery is more than the absence of substance use. What, then, are health, psychological well-being, and recovery? It is true that research has focused little attention on this question; these were fields of healing, not optimizing one's lived experience. As a result, we know a lot about what recovery and mental health *are not* rather than what they *are*. Traditionally, recovery meant living one's life according to the Twelve Steps, indeed a blueprint for a grounded and meaningful life. Millions of people have found both their earthly purpose and a spiritual deliverance by living their lives according to the guidelines of the Steps. Others with substance use problems are already deeply invested in spiritual practices that add meaning to their lives; for these people, their drug use is seen as a distraction from their calling. But what about those who don't believe in the Twelve Steps, the concept of a Higher Power, or the idea that there even is such a thing as a predestined calling? What is the concept of recovery for a gay man who eschews spiritual dimensions to his life? Since so many gay men avoid any involvement with spiritual trappings or the acceptance of a "Higher Power," what can they do to create a meaningful and satisfying life?

The longer your loved one has engaged in a drug-abusing lifestyle, the less likely it is that he has examined the question of a meaningful life. In fact, he may have used substances to hide from the question "What should I be doing with my life?" Or, using the earlier quote, what is an "entirely new and far better life" for a gay man once he stops his substance use and other addictive behaviors (often of a sexual nature)?

Let's look first at what this new and better life is not—one filled with as much pleasure as possible—a goal that research tells us is a dead end.

## PASSING PLEASURES

Many people, particularly those with serious substance abuse problems, lead their lives believing that a good life means having more positive experiences than negative ones. Or, in the words of Martin Seligman and Mihaly Csikszentmihalyi, preeminent psychologists who study the state of happiness, "A simple hedonic calculus suggests that by adding up a person's positive events in consciousness, subtracting the negatives, and aggregating over time, one will get a sum that represents that person's overall well-being."[6]

Based on such a belief, if your loved one can achieve far many more positive experiences (with substance and sexual adventures likely topping the list) than negative consequences throughout his lifetime, he could be said to have lived a satisfying life. This, of course, is rubbish, and even Seligman deflates this appealing but ultimately invalid wish. A good hour, a good day, and even a good week might be based on a ratio of positive to negative during the time frame, but most certainly does not amount to a good life.

Striving to maximize the number of pleasurable experiences ultimately fails to create a satisfying life. Researchers have repeatedly found that "if people seek ecstasy much of the time, whether it be in a career or a love relationship, they are likely to be disappointed. Even worse, they may move to the next relationship or job, seeking intense levels of happiness, which in fact are rarely long-lasting and not necessary for happiness . . . highly pleasurable experiences may have the disadvantage of serving as a contrast point against which to compare other positive experiences, thus making the mild events less pleasurable."[7] Just as with drug use, we adapt to intense pleasures in life and thus need even more for satisfaction. Intense drug-free experiences also cause other calmer activities to appear bland and boring, and certainly not ones your loved one will seek out. Finally, moments of ecstasy do not last long.

## LAYING THE GROUNDWORK

In his best-selling book *Healing the Addicted Brain*, Harold Urschel writes, "The new pressures of living as a sober person can mount quickly, while the new pleasures may come much more slowly. Learning to enjoy life again can be a trial-and-error process that takes time, and we don't always know where to begin. . . . To get back on the road to happiness, you'll first need to acknowledge that your current strategies for finding happiness aren't working and that it's time to make smarter choices."[8]

The groundwork for creating a satisfying drug-free life begins with an acknowledgment that a drug-abusing lifestyle is not really quite as joyous and meaningful as your loved one once believed. He may have entered a period of abstinence to please you, as a requirement of the legal system, to hold on to a job, or because life was becoming generally unmanageable. But a commitment to *lifelong change* seems impossible when substance use is readily available, or, in the words of Robert Du-Pont, recognized trailblazer in the field of addiction treatment, founding director of NIDA, and drug czar under Presidents Nixon and Ford, "I see plenty of people in the grip of addiction, caught in an abusive love affair with a chemical. Like anyone caught in an abusive relationship, they want to believe they can go back to their lover and that the next time, they will work it out."[9]

## Completing a Personal Inventory

This is where a personal inventory, an intervention borrowed from the Twelve Step philosophy, is needed. Indeed, Step Four necessitates a "searching and fearless moral inventory" of oneself. In NIDA's *Therapy Manuals for Drug Addictions,* the need for a personal inventory is highlighted regardless of whether one is working the Twelve Steps or not. In such an inventory, the recovering person honestly examines the impact of substance use on his life and then shares this personal inventory with at least one other person. In fact, Step Five of the Twelve Steps *urges* that this inventory be shared.

The two most common questions that initiate a personal inventory are:

- How did my drug use affect me—physically, emotionally, spiritually, financially, and self-image?

- How did my addiction affect those around me—at home, at work, financially, in social situations, sexually, with regard to the safety of myself and others?

Completing a personal inventory is not a onetime event. Rather, inventories are conducted several times throughout recovery, each time with increasing insight. As a clinician, I have witnessed gay men begin an initial personal inventory and conclude that inventory with superficial responses. This was not due to a lack of trying but rather a lack of insight. As your loved one progresses in his recovery, he will learn more about himself, his motivations, and the far-reaching impact of his drug use on those who love him.

## Examining Character Defects

Creating a meaningful life also requires the acknowledgment of your loved one's "character defects," qualities about himself that he might like to change. Certainly you could name many of his behaviors that you think he should change, especially his substance use. You've probably already told him many times that you're upset about these personal qualities and resulting behaviors.

Here are some of the most common personal characteristics he might show: easily angered, overcritical, easily bored, exploitative, dishonest, self-centered, impatient, overconfident, or low self-esteem. Some of these characteristics pre-date his substance abuse, and others may be consequences of his use. Many men who abuse substances have always had problems with anger and self-centeredness, and have a very low threshold for boredom. It is these very same characteristics that may have led to their initial use. And during their drug-abusing days, they certainly weren't able to work on improving these concerns; indeed, they likely became worse. The times of active substance abuse and early recovery are not good times for him to attempt major character change; there is simply too much going on. However, once he has reached a stable point in his recovery, he can prioritize those that are in his best interest to change, and make a commitment to rid himself of them.

For many gay men, sexual orientation often tops their personal list of character defects. When I encounter such scenarios (and they are common), I remind them and their families that sexual orientation is not a character defect and, regardless, cannot be changed. I've even had gay men argue this point with me; they believe that their orientation is the overpowering defect of their entire being. Learning to accept and embrace one's sexuality is a process that will not be resolved because I tell a gay man that he really is okay and has no reason to be ashamed of his identity. I simply pass over the entire issue by reminding them that the current focus is on character defects that can be changed and modified. All the while I help him to slowly address the internalized heterosexism that plagues every day of his life.

# SPIRITUALITY

People often build the foundation of their recovery on appeasing other people in their lives. If your loved one entered treatment to pacify other people, he is destined to be disappointed. For example, one man stopped drinking due to its impact on his job, and for six months things were running smoothly. Then, without warning, he and twenty other employees were laid off, an occurrence that had nothing to do with alcohol use but was instead the result of a weakening economy. From his perspective, this was a rupture of the pact for his recovery. He felt cheated and soon relapsed.

Even the most harmonious relationships have periods of discord. Imagine how your loved one feels when, after achieving abstinence to, in part, please you, you have a major disagreement. He feels cheated; life was supposed to improve after he stopped drinking. Let's consider Josh's story. He stopped his drug use to rebuild his relationship with his partner, yet months into recovery his partner decided to leave. Josh felt that the ultimate reason for his recovery was gone and so decided that using again didn't seem like a bad move.

At some point addicts recognize the transitory nature of their initial motivations for abstinence. And it is then that they begin to address those existential questions that we must all face at some point in our lives. Why are we here? What is the purpose of my life? And, for addicts in particular, what is the purpose of my experiencing suffering when I can so easily find relief in drugs and alcohol? Why should I stay clean if all of the motivations that compelled me into recovery are fleeting? Big questions abound here, and their answers lead one away from the temporal focus of early recovery into the significance of one's very existence.

Robert DuPont, pioneer in the field of addiction, was asked in a 2010 interview what strategies an addicted person can use to maintain sobriety *over a lifetime*. DuPont replied,

> Not treatment, that is for sure. Treatment is always short-term even at its longest—say a year or two, but more often a month or two. The disease of addiction to alcohol and other drugs, meaning the risk of relapse, is lifelong. Only the growing network of spiritual, religious, and secular recovery fellowships meet that core need of addicted people. Those fellowships are lifelong, matching the disease as nothing else does. . . .

> I see these fellowships as a modern miracle and the key to sustained re-
> covery for most, but not all, addicts to alcohol and other drugs. In fact,
> these programs created the entirely new concept of "recovery," which
> is much more than mere abstinence. The 12-step fellowships support a
> new and better way of life. They are about character as much as about
> abstinence.[10]

While many believe that the very best conduit for spiritual growth
is Twelve Step engagement, even DuPont left room for additional routes
for such growth. In his exemplary book *Thinking Simply about Addiction*, Richard Sandor devotes one-quarter of the text to spiritual development.[11] However he, too, refrains from the use of the word "God" for
those who refuse to participate in Twelve Steps.

If your loved one is able to make use of a Twelve Step group in recovery, the task of spiritual development may be easier for him. Spiritual
practices and/or organized religion for those in recovery are often (but
not always, as we shall soon see) positive forces in recovery. One of the
most robust findings of psychology is that those who actively engaged in
spiritual practices and believe there is a purpose for their existence—one
designed by a Higher Power—are more satisfied with their lives.

You may be tempted to suggest to your loved one that he at least explore a religious service or begin some form of spiritual quest. Such an
approach, however, may be decidedly wrong for some gay men. Some gay
men begin to get their lives back together and re-enter a faith community
after an absence of many years. And within weeks of their return they
are overwhelmed with heterosexist expectations in addition to diatribes
against homosexuality. This is not going to help him with his recovery
and will likely do even more harm. Many organized religions—even those
that preach against homosexuality—have splinter groups that offer spiritual sustenance to gay men. Dignity, an offshoot of the Catholic Church,
is one of those groups. Yet even in these settings, many of the other gay
men your loved one will meet will be ashamed and seeking forgiveness
for their homosexuality. These are not positive role models, particularly if
your loved one's own internalized heterosexism is a source of distress in
his life. An affirmative spiritual practice does not demand gay men seek
forgiveness for their lives but instead celebrates their existence.

Please check your motivation for supporting your loved one's church
attendance. Is it so he will be awakened to his own failings regarding

sexuality? Is it because you are hoping he will change his orientation? If so, you are inadvertently setting him up for failure. On the other hand, if it is to help him find direction and meaning in his life without being condemned for his sexuality, you are on the right track.

## POSITIVE PSYCHOLOGY

For those who absolutely refuse to explore anything but secular options and those who doubt spiritual dimensions, I strongly suggest they seek out material on positive psychology, a relatively new discipline that has shifted the field of psychology away from amelioration of mental illness toward the creation of a satisfying and happy life. The goal is not to be less miserable but rather to live a joyful, authentic, and meaningful life. Researchers investigating positive psychology have come up with some surprising empirically validated findings. Though this research offers fascinating potential for those in recovery, there has thus far been little momentum to combine the two. Addiction research has focused primarily on stabilization and abstinence with an expectation that the Twelve Step programs and organized religions or other spiritual practices would kick in and guide a search for meaning.

One finding from positive psychology that tends to fly in the face of current societal expectations is that money and personal possessions have minimal impact on one's happiness in life. While we've been told this in the past, we now have impressive psychological research to bolster and offer evidence to what is otherwise a strictly moral sentiment. As with substance abuse and intense positive emotions, the thrill of personal acquisition passes quickly, leading one wanting more for the same effect.

Positive psychology research has identified the following as contributing to a happy, satisfying life:

- Build a rich social network.

- Engage in a healthy, supportive relationship.

- Learn to "forgive and forget" past transgressions, both your own and those of others, to increase life satisfaction. Holding on to bitterness detracts from overall happiness.

- Learn to be hopeful and optimistic about the future. There is a good argument for both letting go of the past *and* thinking optimistically about the future. Optimism is not painting unrealistically rosy pictures of the future but is instead a skill that can be learned and mastered. It adds more satisfaction to your life in the present and also leads you to make more effort to change your future for the best.

- Strive to have good days. Increase your positive experiences from mild to moderate intensity (with an occasional roller-coaster ride or bungee jump for thrill seekers)—this will add to feelings of joy in your life. This includes activities that can be done with others and those that can be performed in solitude (I've had more than one man tell me that much of his recovery success stems from Sudoku puzzles). Learn to become more mindful of these pleasures. Slow down and savor the pleasures of enjoyable activities—this helps tilt your days toward the pleasurable.

- Seek out moments of flow. The concept of flow was the basis of a best-selling book a decade ago. Engaging in activities that lead to flow add joy to life. Flow involves activities that require intense concentration in which your senses of time and self vanish. "When does time stop for you? When do you find yourself doing exactly what you want to be doing, and never wanting it to end? Is it painting, or making love, or playing volleyball, or talking before a group, or rock climbing, or listening sympathetically to someone else's troubles?"[12]

I enter moments of flow when writing; I look up at my clock and am amazed to find that hours have passed in what seemed like the blink of an eye. There is now no doubt that the more experiences of flow a person has in life, the more satisfied he is with his life. For many people with substance abuse problems, the only moments of flow come when they are using drugs, and thus they need help to identify substitute activities. And for gay male substance abusers, the most abundant moments of flow involve sex and drug use.

Positive psychology also focuses on identifying individual strengths. Martin Seligman, the recognized leader of the positive psychology movement and former president of the American Psychological Association, writes that there are twenty-four strengths (personality traits) found in various combinations in all human beings.[13] Each one of us has several signature strengths—those traits that typify our personality—that give us pleasure and satisfaction when we are able to put them to use. For example, after taking an inventory of my personality strengths, I found that I scored high for "love of learning," "curiosity and interest in the world," and "fairness and equity." When I am able to participate in activities that call upon my personal signature strengths, I find great joy and happiness, the desired outcomes of positive psychology.

According to Seligman's research, "Happiness, the goal of Positive Psychology, is not just about obtaining momentary subjective states. Happiness also includes the idea that one's life has been authentic . . . authenticity describes the act of deriving gratification and positive emotion from the exercise of one's signature strengths."[14] He also describes a meaningful life as using one's signature strengths in the service of something much larger than one's own life.

Readers interested in identifying their own signature strengths are directed to visit www.authentichappiness.org, the website for positive psychology. When the time is right, you can also direct your loved one to this resource.

## THE ROLE OF SEXUALITY IN ONE'S LIFE

The final stage of development of a positive identity as a sexual minority is called identity synthesis. By the time your loved one has reached this stage, he has worked through grief, shame, and anger. Being a gay man is an important part of his identity, but not his entire identity. He recognizes that no matter what society may think about his sexuality, he is okay with himself.

Do gay men want to mimic the lives of heterosexuals or create their own gay-specific lifestyles? Many gay men consider their sexual orientation as unremarkable and want others to approach them the same way; other gay men have created a culture that accentuates their orientation. Neither group is wrong, but your loved one will feel a tension between these two poles. Only your loved one can ultimately envision and build a life that gives him meaning and joy. However, gay culture's often incessant focus on sex, substance use, physical perfection, and instant gratification will be constant distractions as he attempts to define the role of his sexual orientation in his life.

Just as your loved one is exploring his sexual identity, society as a whole is considering the role and value of gay men and women. At the writing of this book, lawsuits are occurring across the country in regard to gay marriage, and the Department of Defense is deciding how to implement changes now that the policy "don't ask, don't tell" has been overturned. Society recognizes that gay individuals are not some alien species that needs to be quarantined or at least sequestered. There is without doubt a long battle ahead, but sexual minorities are increasingly recognized as neighbors, workmates, family members, close friends, and part of the tapestry of our lives. The gay community is undergoing its own self-exploration; does it want to be defined by shallow pursuits, or is there so much more unearthed potential? A gay culture that continuously pursues transient and shallow pleasures may be a turnoff or diversion for a gay man struggling to define his life after he ends or reduces his substance use.

::

The three primary goals for involved family members of a substance-abusing gay male are advocating for his care, ending enabling, and minimizing shame-inducing and rejecting interactions. Whether you're a parent, spouse/partner, or close friend, or assume any other role that is part of your loved one's family constellation, please recall the following:

1. Advocacy. It is no secret that accessing state-of-the-art substance abuse treatment is challenging, but if the person seeking services is a gay man, his options are even more limited. Most facilities have limited experience in working with gay men, and providers have minimal knowledge of this population and even a minimal desire to work with them. It's great if he can afford a gay-specific facility, but most will access more affordable and convenient treatment options. Please use the information in this book to ensure that your loved one is working with a person and/or treatment facility that is proficient with both substance abuse and gay male sexual issues.

2. Decrease enabling. Any behaviors on your part that subtly encourage continued drug use or that allow him to avoid the consequences of this use ultimately allow a progression of the problem.

To end enabling behaviors, request change and detail the consequences if his drug use continues; increase the number of negative
consequences that occur when drug use happens; and increase the
positive consequences when it doesn't. Family members need to take
care of and protect themselves no matter what the drug user does.

3. Decrease shameful and rejecting behaviors. The Family Acceptance Project (FAP) is a research, intervention, education, and
policy initiative directed by Dr. Caitlin Ryan and affiliated with
San Francisco State University. FAP studies how family acceptance
and rejection affect the health, mental health, and well-being of
lesbian, gay, bisexual, and transgender (LGBT) youth. This research
finds, in short, that families really matter! In fact, this research
shows that families have a compelling impact on their LGBT children's health and mental health, including drug use. FAP found
that the more rejecting family members were, the more severe the
health and mental health outcomes for the LGBT youth. Dr. Ryan
and her research team identified more than fifty specific parental
and caregiver behaviors that express rejection of their LGBT children. They linked each of these rejecting behaviors with specific
health and mental health concerns. Some of these family rejecting
behaviors include:

- hitting, slapping, or physically hurting a child because of
  their LGBT identity

- verbal harassment or name-calling because of a child's
  LGBT identity

- excluding LGBT youth from family events and family
  activities

- blocking access to LGBT friends, events, and resources

- blaming a child when they are discriminated against
  because of their LGBT identity

- pressuring a child to be more (or less) masculine or
  feminine

- telling a child that God will punish them because they
  are gay

- telling a child that the parent/caregiver is ashamed of them or that how they look or act will shame the family

- making a child keep their LGBT identity a secret in the family and not letting them talk about their identity with others[15]

When I first read this list, I was stunned. *While FAP's focus is on youth, all of these behaviors are evident in the families of even adult gay men.* Too many gay men grew up with rejecting behaviors in their families and continue to do so even into adulthood. These family interactions in no way support your loved one as he works toward reducing or ending his substance use. Of course, some families have been very supportive of their loved one from their early years, and yet these men still ended up with a substance abuse problem.

Other primary causes of substance abuse and dependence examined in this book were genetics, peer influence, and the stigma of living as a gay man in a society that still does not accept this identity. Recall that not all gay male substance abusers are ashamed of their identity, and behavioral interventions and support may suffice for change, but for those who are, coming to terms with sexuality will be a long-term endeavor on which recovery teeters.

FAP researchers also identified and measured the health and mental health impact of more than fifty family accepting behaviors. Some of these include:

- talking with a child or foster child about their LGBT identity

- supporting a child's LGBT identity even though you may feel uncomfortable

- advocating for a child when he or she is mistreated because of their identity

- requiring that other family members respect an LGBT child

- bringing a child to LGBT organizations or events

- working to make a congregation supportive of LGBT members, or finding a supportive faith community that welcomes the family and LGBT child

- welcoming a child's LGBT friends and partner to the home and to family events and activities

- believing that an LGBT child can have a happy life[16]

Psychological health requires that we fold our sexuality into our identity. Your loved one, then, must eventually ponder the significance and meaning of living as a gay male. If he cannot accept and incorporate this into his identity, his chance of relapse is very high, he risks the brittle existence of a "dry drunk" or "clean addict," or he substitutes one addiction for another, likely substances for sex.

Your loved one will experience many changes as he works his way through the critical stage of early recovery, but one aspect that will not change is his sexuality. Please recognize that for many gay men, wrestling with sexuality will be the most daunting task they perform in their recovery. In the early stages of recovery, your loved one will be pleased just to see a reduction in substance use, but he'll need to come to grips with his sexuality to continually improve and attain psychological health.

# AFTERWORD

WHILE TWENTY-TWO MILLION AMERICANS are in need of substance abuse treatment, only two million access this help each year. Furthermore, 94 percent of those needing help don't even recognize their need for treatment—at least not yet.[1] Thus how many gay men do not even recognize that they are on their way to developing a substance abuse problem—or have already developed one—due to the norm of substance use in the community?

Though it has often been assumed that gay men abuse drugs mainly as a way of coping with the shame connected to internalized homophobia, recent research finds that the dearth of social outlets for these men that are alcohol and drug free is just as predictive. In most social settings, when gay men get together, the event requires some form of substance with addictive potential. Even men who are quite comfortable with their sexuality and have little to no internalized homophobia can develop substance abuse problems due to its excessive presence in the community. Indeed, the superabundance of addictive substances in gay and bisexual communities not only increases the likelihood of gay men developing a substance abuse problem, but also makes recovery efforts more difficult.

Sadly, those with a substance abuse problem are often the very last to recognize that their drug use has escalated to problematic abuse, dependence, or addiction. Robert DuPont, one of the world's leaders in addiction research and a scholar who has been quoted frequently in this book, believes that one of the defining characteristics of addiction is dishonesty to oneself and others about the severity of one's use.[2] It is often loved ones and concerned others who are the first to notice the specter of drug abuse.

Once a recovery or moderate use effort is undertaken by a gay man, either voluntarily or through family, legal, and/or employment demands, there are five possible outcomes:

1. Abstinence: He refrains from all substance use.

2. Non-problematic use: He learns to engage in moderate and controlled substance use which minimizes the myriad risks to himself (and others).

3. Slow improvement: For these men, an intervention for substance abuse does not yield immediate positive results. However, they do show slow and gradual improvements in their lives, possibly achieving abstinence in the end.

4. Worsening use over time: Many who initially succeed in their goal of either attenuating or ending all substance use then go on to relapse or begin a gradual descent back to substance abuse.

5. Lack of success: These individuals have no success in changing their substance use patterns.

The families of gay men most certainly desire abstinence—or at least non-problematic use or slow improvement—as an outcome. To achieve this, gay men will have to work on issues common to all individuals seeking help for substance abuse as well as issues most relevant to their own demographic, including internalized heterosexism, shame, the co-occurrence of sexual activity and drug use, a meaning of life that may avoid traditional spiritual dimensions, and the development of sober and clean leisure and social outlets in a community in which their availability is sparse. Simultaneously, loved ones will decrease enabling, shameful, and rejecting behaviors, and advocate for the gay man's care.

This book has covered all of the aforementioned topics, but by no means has this text covered all possible issues. For example, much of what we know about gay men and their treatment for substance abuse is based on white gay men. The National Alliance on Mental Illness (NAMI) reports that most mental health research on the GLBT population has used primarily white samples and that there is scant research and services for racial and ethnic minorities, rural populations, bisexuals, transgender individuals, and those with serious mental health issues.[3] When we factor in ethnicity, age, HIV status, rural/urban environment, and the host of other factors that affect each and every gay man seeking help for his drug use problem, we begin to understand the complexity of treatment and the obstacles impeding recovery for our client or loved one.

While we have a lot of work ahead of us, there is an increasing inter-est in treating gay men, and a holistic approach beckons on the distant horizon. But for now, we must do what we can, sometimes facilitating miracles in spite of our rudimentary knowledge. Treatment profession-als, family members, and gay men themselves must continually advocate for improvement in research and treatment as well as actively work to destigmatize same-sex sexual orientation and desire so that the shame that anchors the lives of so many gay men never has the opportunity to fasten itself to new generations of gay men.

# RESOURCES

## Books

Anderson, S. *Substance Abuse Disorders in Lesbian, Gay, Bisexual, and Transgender Clients.* New York: Columbia University Press, 2009.

Carnes, P. *A Gentle Path through the Twelve Steps.* Center City, MN: Hazelden, 1993.

Center for Substance Abuse Treatment. *A Provider's Introduction to Substance Abuse Treatment for Lesbian, Gay, Bisexual, and Transgender Individuals.* Rockville, MD: U.S. Department of Health and Human Services, 2001.

Finnegan, D. G., and E. B. McNally. *Counseling Lesbian, Gay, Bisexual, and Transgender Substance Abusers.* New York: Haworth Press, 2002.

Greenan, D., and G. Tunnell. *Couple Therapy with Gay Men.* New York: Guilford Press, 2003.

Jay, J., and D. Jay. *Love First: A Family's Guide to Intervention.* Center City, MN: Hazelden, 2008.

Kominars, S. B., and K. D. Kominars. *Accepting Ourselves and Others.* Center City, MN: Hazelden, 1996.

Makadon, H. J., K. H. Mayer, J. Potter, and H. Goldhammer. *The Fenway Guide to Lesbian, Gay, Bisexual, and Transgender Health.* Philadelphia: American College of Physicians, 2008.

Osborne, D. *Suicide Tuesday.* New York: Carroll and Graf Publishers, 2005.

Shelton, M. *Boy Crazy.* New York: Alyson Books, 2008.

Weiss, R. *Cruise Control.* Los Angeles: Alyson Books, 2005.

## Web Sites

**Above the Influence**
This site helps young people understand the dangers of drug use and make responsible decisions about their lives.
www.abovetheinfluence.com

**Authentic Happiness**
A site devoted to the research on happiness and the field of positive psychology.
www.authentichappiness.org

**DanceSafe**
A nonprofit organization promoting health and safety within the rave and night-club community.
www.dancesafe.org

**Gay Party Drug and Crystal Information**
http://lifeormeth.com

**Love First**
A comprehensive site for planning a family intervention.
www.lovefirst.net

**Sex Help**
The web site for Patrick Carnes and his research on sexual addiction. It offers a number of self-tests for sexual addiction.
www.sexhelp.com

**Tweaker.org**
A site targeting gay men who use drugs and alcohol with an emphasis on sexual safety.
http://tweaker.org

## Journals

**Journal of Gay and Lesbian Mental Health**
Official Journal of the Association of Gay and Lesbian Psychiatrists
www.informaworld.com/smpp/title-content=t792304010-db=all

## Organizations

**Al-Anon**
1600 Corporate Landing Parkway
Virginia Beach, VA 23454-5617
(757) 563-1600
www.al-anon.alateen.org

**Alcoholics Anonymous**
P.O. Box 459
New York, NY 10163
(212) 870-3400
www.aa.org

**American Psychological Association's Division 44**
Society for the Psychological Study of Lesbian, Gay, Bisexual, and Transgender Issues
A division of the American Psychological Association.
www.apadivision44.org

**Association of Gay and Lesbian Psychiatrists**
4514 Chester Ave.
Philadelphia, PA 19143-3707
(215) 222-2800
www.aglp.org

**Cocaine Anonymous**
21720 S. Wilmington Ave., Ste. 304
Long Beach, CA 90810-1641
(310) 559-5833
www.ca.org

**The Family Acceptance Project**
This community research, intervention, and education initiative studies the impact
of family acceptance and rejection on the physical health, mental health, and well-
being of lesbian, gay, bisexual, and transgender (LGBT) youth.
San Francisco State University
3004 16th Street, #301
San Francisco, CA 94103
http://familyproject.sfsu.edu

**The Gay and Lesbian Medical Association**
Gay and Lesbian Medical Association
459 Fulton Street, Suite 107
San Francisco, CA 94102
(415) 255-4547
www.glma.org

**Human Rights Campaign**
The Human Rights Campaign is America's largest civil rights organization working to achieve lesbian, gay, bisexual, and transgender (LGBT) equality. It seeks to
improve the lives of LGBT Americans by advocating for equal rights and benefits
in the workplace, ensuring families are treated equally under the law and increasing public support among all Americans through innovative advocacy, education,
and outreach programs. HRC works to secure equal rights for LGBT individuals
and families at the federal and state levels by lobbying elected officials, mobilizing
grassroots supporters, educating Americans, investing strategically to elect fair-
minded officials, and partnering with other LGBT organizations.
1640 Rhode Island Ave NW
Washington, DC 20036-3278
(202) 628-4160
www.hrc.org

**International Advisory Council for Homosexual Men and Women in Alcoholics
Anonymous (IAC)**
The International Advisory Council (IAC) serves the gay and lesbian members of
Alcoholics Anonymous. Its purpose is to provide experience, strength, and hope to
any arm of AA.
9226 Barr Circle
Houston, TX 77080
www.iac-aa.org

**International Service Organization of COSA**
COSA is a Twelve Step recovery program for men and women whose lives have
been affected by another person's compulsive sexual behavior.
P.O. Box 14537
Minneapolis, MN 55414
(763) 537-6904
www.cosa-recovery.org

**Narcotics Anonymous**
P.O. Box 9999
Van Nuys, CA 91409
(818) 773-9999
www.na.org

**National Alliance on Mental Illness**
3803 N. Fairfax Dr., Ste. 100
Arlington, VA 22203
(703) 524-7600
www.nami.org

**National Association of Lesbian, Gay Bisexual,
and Transgender Addiction Professionals**
1001 N. Fairfax Street
Suite 201
Alexandria, VA 22314
www.nalgap.org

**Parents, Families, and Friends of Lesbians and Gays (PFLAG)**
PFLAG promotes the health and well-being of lesbian, gay, bisexual,
and transgender persons, their families, and friends.
1828 L Street NW
Suite 660
Washington, DC 20036
(202) 467-8180
www.pflag.org

**Pride Institute**
Pride Institute is committed to providing lesbian, gay, bisexual, and transgender
people a road to recovery through evidence-based substance abuse, sexual health,
and mental health treatment.
14400 Martin Drive
Eden Prairie, MN 55344
952-934-7554
(800) 547-7433
www.pride-institute.com

**Secular Organizations for Sobriety (SOS)**
4773 Hollywood Blvd.
Hollywood, CA 90027
(323) 666-4295
www.cfiwest.org/sos/index.htm

**Self Management and Recovery Training (SMART)**
7304 Mentor Avenue, Suite F
Mentor, OH 44060
(866) 951-5357
(440) 951-5357
www.smartrecovery.org

**Sex Addicts Anonymous**
ISO of SAA
P.O. Box 70949
Houston, TX 77270
(800) 477-8191
www.sexaa.org

**Sexaholics Anonymous**
P.O. Box 3565
Brentwood, TN 37024
(615) 370-6062
(866) 424-8777
www.sa.org

**Sex and Love Addicts Anonymous**
Fellowship-Wide Services
1550 NE Loop 410, Ste 118
San Antonio, TX 78209
(210) 828-7900
www.slaafws.org

**Sexual Compulsives Anonymous**
P.O. Box 1585, Old Chelsea Station
New York, NY 10011
(800) 977-HEAL (4325)
www.sca-recovery.org

**Sexuality Information and Education Council of the United States**
Provides education and information about sexuality and sexual and reproductive
health.
1706 R Street NW
Washington, DC 20009
(202) 265-2405
www.siecus.org/

## Religious Groups

**DignityUSA (Catholic)**
P.O. Box 376
Medford, MA 02155
(800) 877-8797
(202) 861-0017
www.dignityusa.org

**Integrity (Episcopal)**
620 Park Avenue, #311
Rochester, NY 14607-2943
(800) 462-9498
(585) 360-4512
www.integrityusa.org

**Metropolitan Community Churches (Christian)**
P.O. Box 1374
Abilene, TX 79604
(310) 360-8640
http://ufmcc.com/

# Notes

## Chapter One

1. Peter R. Martin, Bennett Alan Weinberg, and Bonnie K. Bealer, *Healing Addiction* (Hoboken, NJ: John Wiley and Sons, 2007), 24–25.
2. Jennifer P. Schneider, "Coexisting Disorders," in *Addiction Counseling Review*, ed. R. H. Coombs (Mahwah, NJ: Lawrence Erlbaum Associates, 2005).
3. National Institute on Drug Abuse, *The Science of Addiction* (Bethesda, MD: National Institutes of Health, 2007), 5.
4. G. Mansergh, D. W. Purcell, R. Stall, M. McFarlane, S. Semaan, J. Valentine, and R. Valdiserri, "CDC Consultation on Methamphetamine Use and Sexual Risk Behavior for HIV/STD Infection: Summary and Suggestions," *Public Health Reports* 121 (2006): 127–132.
5. Perry N. Halkitis, "The Impact of Crystal Amphetamine Use on HIV-Positive Individuals," *POZ* (2009): 1–4.
6. Christopher Heredia, "The Dance of Death," *San Francisco Chronicle,* May 4, 2003, A1.
7. P. N. Halkitis, T. Parsons, R. J. Wolitski, and R. H. Remien, "Characteristics of HIV Antiretroviral Treatments, Access and Adherence in an Ethnically Diverse Sample of Men Who Have Sex With Men," *Aids Care* 15 (2003): 89–102.
8. Carlo C. DiClemente, *Addiction and Change* (New York: Guilford Press, 2003), 101.
9. Alcoholics Anonymous, *Alcoholics Anonymous*, 3rd ed. (New York: Alcoholics Anonymous World Services, 1976), 31.

## Chapter Two

1. Sandra Anderson, personal correspondence, Jan. 31, 2010.
2. Michael Muller, "NIDA-Funded Studies Shed Light on Neurobiology of Drug Craving," *NIDA Notes* 11 (1996): 4.
3. L. B. Cottler, S. B. Womack, W. M. Compton, and A. Ben-Abdallah, "Ecstasy Abuse and Dependence Among Adolescents and Young Adults: Applicability and Reliability of DSM-IV Criteria," *Human Psychopharmacology* 16 (2001): 599–606.
4. A. L. Stone, C. L. Storr, and J. C. Anthony, "Evidence for a Hallucinogen Dependence Syndrome Developing Soon After Onset of Hallucinogen Use During Adolescence," *International Journal of Methods in Psychiatric Research* 15 (2006): 116–30.
5. Duncan Osborne, *Suicide Tuesday* (New York: Carroll and Graf Publishers, 2005), v.

6. L. Whitten, "Treatment Curbs Methamphetamine Abuse among Gay and Bisexual Men," *NIDA Notes* 20 (2006): 4.
7. National Institute on Drug Abuse, *Topics in Brief: Methamphetamine Addiction: Cause for Concern—Hope for the Future* (Bethesda, MD: National Institutes of Health, 2007).
8. Tweaker.org: www.tweaker.org/html/life/whywedolists/whywedo.html. Used with permission.
9. J. A. Bauermeister, "It's All About 'Connecting': Reasons for Drug Use among Latino Gay Men Living in the San Francisco Bay Area," *Journal of Ethnicity in Substance Abuse* 6 (2007): 109–29.
10. Tweaker.org: www.tweaker.org/html/crystalsex/cmsex.html. Used with permission.
11. Joseph Couture, *Peek: Inside the Private World of Public Sex* (New York: Routledge, 2008), 105.
12. Robert Weiss, *Cruise Control* (Los Angeles: Alyson Books, 2005).

## Chapter Three

1. Center for Substance Abuse Treatment, *A Provider's Introduction to Substance Abuse Treatment for Lesbian, Gay, Bisexual, and Transgender Individuals* (Rockville, MD: U.S. Department of Health and Human Services, 2001), 7.
2. Sheppard B. Kominars and Kathryn D. Kominars, *Accepting Ourselves and Others* (Center City, MN: Hazelden, 1996).
3. W. Rosario, E. W. Schrimshaw, and J. Hunter, "Predictors of Substance Use Over Time among Gay, Lesbian, and Bisexual Youths: An Examination of Three Hypotheses," *Addictive Behavior* 29 (2004): 1624.
4. Sylvia K. Fisher, "Checklist of Reasons for Drinking for Single Gay and Lesbian Clients," *Counselor* (2002), www.counselormagazine.com/columns-mainmenu-55/41-assessment-tools/448-checklist-of-reasons-for-drinking-for-single-gay-and-lesbian-clients. Reprinted with the permission of Health Communications, Inc., www.hcibooks.com.
5. Robert P. Cabaj, "Substance Abuse, Internalized Homophobia, and Gay Men and Lesbians: Psychodynamic Issues and Clinical Implications," *Journal of Gay and Lesbian Psychotherapy* 3 (2000): 11.

## Chapter Four

1. National Institute on Drug Abuse, *Principles of Drug Addiction Treatment: A Research-Based Guide* (Bethesda, MD: National Institutes of Health, 2009), 2.
2. Barbara S. McCrady, "Family and Other Close Relationships," in *Rethinking Substance Abuse,* ed. W. R. Miller and K. M. Carroll (New York: Guilford Press, 2006).
3. National Institute on Drug Abuse, *Principles of Drug Addiction Treatment.*
4. Center for Substance Abuse Treatment, *A Provider's Introduction.*
5. William R. Miller and Kathleen M. Carroll, "Drawing the Science Together," in *Rethinking Substance Abuse,* ed. W. R. Miller and K. M. Carroll (New York: Guilford Press, 2006).

6. Tweaker.org: www.tweaker.org/html/life/useabuse.html. Used with permission.
7. Jeff Jay and Debra Jay, "Introduction to Intervention," www.lovefirst.net/ xarticles/article3.htm.
8. Ibid.
9. Jeff Jay and Debra Jay, *Love First: A Family's Guide to Intervention* (Center City, MN: Hazelden, 2008).
10. Joseph Nowinski and Stuart Baker, *The Twelve-Step Facilitation Handbook* (San Francisco: Jossey-Bass, 1992), 159.
11. Ibid., 109.
12. Harold C. Urschel, *Healing the Addicted Brain* (Naperville, IL: Sourcebooks, 2009), 207.
13. Thomas McLellan, "What We Need Is a System," in *Rethinking Substance Abuse,* ed. W. R. Miller and K. M. Carroll (New York: Guilford Press, 2006), 290.

## Chapter Five

1. Center for Substance Abuse Treatment, *A Provider's Introduction.*
2. Candy Finnigan, *When Enough Is Enough* (New York: Avery, 2008), 155.

## Chapter Six

1. American Psychological Association, "Guidelines for Psychotherapy with Lesbian, Gay, and Bisexual Clients," *American Psychologist* 55 (2000).
2. Center for Substance Abuse Treatment, *A Provider's Introduction.*
3. Personal correspondence, March 4, 2010.
4. Vivienne Cass, "Homosexual Identity Formation: A Theoretical Model," *Journal of Homosexuality* 4 (1979).
5. Dana G. Finnegan and Emily B. McNally, *Counseling Lesbian, Gay, Bisexual, and Transgender Substance Abusers* (New York: Haworth Press, 2002), 169.
6. Daniel Goleman, *Emotional Intelligence* (New York: Bantam Books, 1995).
7. National Institute on Drug Abuse, *Therapy Manuals for Drug Addiction: A Cognitive-Behavioral Approach: Treating Cocaine Addiction* (Bethesda, MD: U.S. Department of Health and Human Services, 1998), 59.

## Chapter Seven

1. Father Leo Booth, "Spirituality and the Gay Community," in *Addiction and Recovery in Gay and Lesbian Persons,* ed. R. J. Kus (New York: Harrington Park Press, 1995).
2. Narcotics Anonymous, *Narcotics Anonymous,* 4th ed. (Van Nuys, CA: Narcotics Anonymous World Services, 1982), 23.
3. Penny Ziegler, "Addiction Psychiatric Help: The Doctor Is Out," *NALGALP Reporter* 23 (2010): 6.
4. Patrick Carnes, *Facing the Shadow* (Carefree, AZ: Gentle Path Press, 2008), 277.
5. Robert J. Kus and Mark A. Latcovich, "Special Interest Groups in Alcoholics Anonymous: A Focus on Gay Men's Groups," in *Addiction and Recovery in Gay and Lesbian Persons,* ed. R. J. Kus (New York: Harrington Park Press, 1995).
6. Urschel, *Healing the Addicted Brain,* 114.

## Chapter Eight

1. Alan Deutschman, *Change or Die* (New York: HarperCollins, 2007), 3.
2. National Institute on Drug Abuse, *Science of Addiction*, 5.
3. Daniel Gilbert, *Stumbling on Happiness* (New York: Knopf, 2006), 106 and 114.
4. Sandor, *Thinking Simply about Addiction* (New York: Jeremy P. Tarcher/ Penguin, 2009), 92.
5. Ori Brafman and Rom Brafman, *Sway* (New York: Broadway, 2008), 180.
6. Urschel, *Healing the Addicted Brain*, 210.
7. National Institute on Drug Abuse, *Therapy Manuals for Drug Addiction: An Individual Counseling Approach to Treat Cocaine Addiction* (Bethesda, MD: U.S. Department of Health and Human Services, 1998); Dennis M. Donovan, "Assessment of Addictive Behaviors for Relapse Prevention," in *Assessment of Addictive Behaviors*, ed. D. M. Donovan and G. A. Marlatt (New York: Guilford Press, 2005); Mary M. Velasquez, Gaylyn G. Maurer, Cathy Crouch, and Carlo C. DiClemente, *Group Treatment for Substance Abuse* (New York: Guilford Press, 2001).

## Chapter Nine

1. Sandor, *Thinking Simply about Addiction*, 86–87.
2. Avram Goldstein, *Addiction: From Biology to Drug Policy* (New York: W. H. Freeman and Company, 1994), 115–16.
3. Conference on Approaches for Combating the Troublesome Use of Substances (CACTUS), described in *Rethinking Substance Abuse*, ed. W. R. Miller and K. M. Carroll (New York: Guilford Press, 2006), xii.
4. Deborah Hasin, Mark Hatzenbuehler, and Rachel Waxman, "Genetics of Substance Use Disorders," in *Rethinking Substance Abuse*, ed. W. R. Miller and K. M. Carroll (New York: Guilford Press, 2006), 75.
5. DiClemente, *Addiction and Change*, 142–43.
6. Edward Rubin, "Integration of Theory, Research, and Practice: A Clinician's Perspective," in *Treating Substance Abuse*, ed. F. Rotgers, J. Morgenstern, and S. T. Walters (New York: Guilford Press, 2003), 353.

## Chapter Ten

1. Sexuality Information and Education Council of the United States, *Guidelines for Comprehensive Sexuality Education* (New York: SIECUS, 2004).
2. Center for Substance Abuse Treatment, *A Provider's Introduction*, 83.
3. Finnegan and McNally, *Counseling Lesbian, Gay, Bisexual, and Transgender Substance Abusers*, 142–43.

## Chapter Eleven

1. SAMHSA, "National Registry of Evidence-based Programs and Practices (NREPP)," www.nrepp.samhsa.gov.

2. Timothy J. O'Farrell, and William Fals-Stewart, *Behavioral Couples Therapy for Alcoholism and Drug Abuse* (New York: Guilford Press, 2006).

3. Ibid., 99.

## Chapter Twelve

1. Richard Sandor, *Thinking Simply about Addiction,* 33–34.

2. Ibid., 138.

3. Martin E. Seligman and Mihaly Csikszentmihalyi, "Positive Psychology: An Introduction," *American Psychologist* 55 (2000): 5.

4. Christopher Peterson, "The Future of Optimism," *American Psychologist* 55 (2000): 50.

5. White, "Interviews with Pioneers," *Counselor* 11 (2010), 48.

6. Seligman and Csikszentmihalyi, "Positive Psychology," 11.

7. Ed Diener, "Subjective Well-Being," *American Psychologist* 55 (2000): 36.

8. Urschel, *Healing the Addicted Brain,* 255 and 256.

9. White, "Interviews with Pioneers," 47.

10. Ibid., 47 and 43.

11. Sandor, *Thinking Simply about Addiction,* chapter 4.

12. Martin E. Seligman, *Authentic Happiness* (New York: Free Press, 2002), 114.

13. Ibid.

14. Ibid., 262.

15. Caitlin Ryan, *Supportive Families, Healthy Children: Helping Families with Lesbian, Gay, Bisexual & Transgender Children* (San Francisco: Marian Wright Edelman Institute, San Francisco State University, 2009), 8.

16. Ibid., 9.

## Afterword

1. Larry M. Gentilello, "More Patients or More Competition," *Addiction Professional* 8 (2010).

2. Robert L. DuPont, *The Selfish Brain: Learning from Addiction* (Center City, MN: Hazelden, 1997).

3. National Alliance on Mental Illness, *Disparities in Mental Health Treatment among GLBT Populations* (Arlington, VA: NAMI, 2007).

# BIBLIOGRAPHY

Alonzo, D. "Working with Same-Sex Couples." In *Handbook of Couples Therapy*, edited by M. Harway, 370–85. Hoboken, NJ: John Wiley and Sons, 2005.

Amadio, D. M. "Internalized Heterosexism, Alcohol Use, and Alcohol-Related Problems among Lesbians and Gay Men." *Addictive Behaviors* 31 (2006): 1153–62.

American Psychiatric Association. *Diagnostic and Statistical Manual of Mental Disorders.* 4th ed., text rev. Washington, DC: American Psychiatric Association, 2000.

American Psychological Association. "Guidelines for Psychotherapy with Lesbian, Gay, and Bisexual Clients." *American Psychologist* 55 (2000): 1440–51.

Anderson, S. *Substance Abuse Disorders in Lesbian, Gay, Bisexual, and Transgender Clients.* New York: Columbia University Press, 2009.

Bauermeister, J. A. "It's All about 'Connecting': Reasons for Drug Use among Latino Gay Men Living in the San Francisco Bay Area." *Journal of Ethnicity in Substance Abuse* 6 (2007): 109–29.

Berzon, B. *Permanent Partners.* New York: Plume, 2004.

Booth, L. "Spirituality and the Gay Community." In *Addiction and Recovery in Gay and Lesbian Persons,* edited by R. J. Kus, 57–65. New York: Harrington Park Press, 1995.

Booth, L. *When God Becomes a Drug: Understanding Religious Addiction and Religious Abuse.* New York: SCP Limited, 1998.

Brafman, O., and R. Brafman. *Sway.* New York: Broadway, 2008.

Brecht, M., A. O'Brien, C. von Mayrhauser, and M. D. Anglin. "Methamphetamine Use Behaviors and Gender Differences." *Addictive Behaviors* 29 (2004): 89–106.

Bux, D. A., and T. W. Irwin. "Combining Motivational Interviewing and Cognitive-Behavioral Skills Training for the Treatment of Crystal Methamphetamine Abuse/Dependence." *Journal of Gay and Lesbian Psychotherapy* 10 (2006): 143–52.

Cabaj, R. P. "Substance Abuse, Internalized Homophobia, and Gay Men and Lesbians: Psychodynamic Issues and Clinical Implications." *Journal of Gay and Lesbian Psychotherapy* 3 (2000): 5–24.

Carnes, P. *Facing the Shadow.* Carefree, AZ: Gentle Path Press, 2008.

Carnes, P. *A Gentle Path through the Twelve Steps*. Center City, MN: Hazelden, 1993.

Cass, V. C. "Homosexual Identity Formation: A Theoretical Model." *Journal of Homosexuality* 4 (1979): 219–35.

Center for Substance Abuse Treatment. *A Provider's Introduction to Substance Abuse Treatment for Lesbian, Gay, Bisexual, and Transgender Individuals.* Rockville, MD: U.S. Department of Health and Human Services, 2001.

Cottler, L. B., S. B. Womack, W. M. Compton, and A. Ben-Abdallah. "Ecstasy Abuse and Dependence among Adolescents and Young Adults: Applicability and Reliability of DSM-IV Criteria." *Human Psychopharmacology* 16 (2001): 599–606.

Couture, J. *Peek: Inside the Private World of Public Sex*. New York: Routledge, 2008.

DiClemente, C. C. *Addiction and Change*. New York: Guilford Press, 2003.

Diener, E. "Subjective Well-Being." *American Psychologist* 55 (2000): 34–43.

Deutschman, A. *Change or Die.* New York: HarperCollins, 2007.

Donovan, D. M. "Assessment of Addictive Behaviors for Relapse Prevention." In *Assessment of Addictive Behaviors,* edited by D. M. Donovan and G. A. Marlatt, 1–48. New York: Guilford Press, 2005.

Donovan, D. M., and G. A. Marlatt. *Assessment of Addictive Behaviors*. New York: Guilford Press, 2005.

Dunkle, J. "Counseling Gay Male Clients: A Review of Treatment Efficacy Research: 1975–Present." *Journal of Gay and Lesbian Psychotherapy* 2 (1994): 1–19.

DuPont, R. L. *The Selfish Brain: Learning from Addiction*. Center City, MN: Hazelden, 1997.

Eisenberg, M., and H. Wechsler. "Substance Use Behaviors among College Students with Same-Sex and Opposite-Sex Experience: Results from a National Study." *Addictive Behaviors* 28 (2003): 899–913.

Finnegan, D. G., and E. B. McNally. *Counseling Lesbian, Gay, Bisexual, and Transgender Substance Abusers*. New York: Haworth Press, 2002.

Finnigan, C. *When Enough Is Enough*. New York: Avery, 2008.

Fisher, S. K. "Checklist of Reasons for Drinking for Single Gay and Lesbian Clients." *Counselor,* March 31, 2002, www.counselormagazine.com/columns-mainmenu-55/41-assessment-tools/448-checklist-of-reasons-for-drinking-for-single-gay-and-lesbian-clients (accessed June 26, 2010).

Gilbert, D. *Stumbling on Happiness*. New York: Knopf, 2006.

Goldstein, A. *Addiction: From Biology to Drug Policy*. New York: W. H. Freeman and Company, 1994.

Goleman, D. *Emotional Intelligence*. New York: Bantam Books, 1995.

Greenan, D., and G. Tunnell. *Couple Therapy with Gay Men*. New York: Guilford Press, 2003.

Halkitis, P. N., T. Parsons, R. J. Wolitski, and R. H. Remien. "Characteristics of HIV Antiretroviral Treatments, Access and Adherence in an Ethnically Diverse Sample of Men Who Have Sex with Men." *Aids Care* 15 (2003): 89–102.

Halkitis, P. N. "The Impact of Crystal Amphetamine Use on HIV-Positive Individuals." *POZ* (2009): 1–4.

Hasin, D., M. Hatzenbuehler, and R. Waxman. "Genetics of Substance Use Disorders." In *Rethinking Substance Abuse,* edited by W. R. Miller and K.M. Carroll, 61–77. New York: Guilford Press, 2006.

Heredia, C. "The Dance of Death." *The San Francisco Chronicle*, May 4, 2003, A1.

Irwin, T. W. "Strategies for the Treatment of Methamphetamine Use Disorders among Gay and Bisexual Men." *Journal of Gay and Lesbian Psychotherapy* 10 (2006): 131–41.

Jay, J., and D. Jay. *Love First: A Family's Guide to Intervention*. Center City, MN: Hazelden, 2008.

Kirchick, J. "Tripping Over a Leg Up." *The Advocate* 1036 (2010): 18–19.

Kominars, S. B., and K. D. Kominars. *Accepting Ourselves and Others*. Center City, MN: Hazelden, 1996.

Kus, R. J. *Addiction and Recovery in Gay and Lesbian Persons*. New York: Harrington Park Press, 1995.

Kus., R. J., and M. A. Latcovich. "Special Interest Groups in Alcoholics Anonymous: A Focus on Gay Men's Groups." In *Addiction and Recovery in Gay and Lesbian Persons,* edited by R. J. Kus, 67–82. New York: Harrington Park Press, 1995.

Langdridge, D. "Gay Affirmative Therapy: A Theoretical Framework and Defense." *Journal of Gay and Lesbian Psychotherapy* 11 (2007): 27–43.

Leiblum, S., and R. Rosen. "Introduction: Changing Perspectives on Sexual Desire." In *Sexual Desire Disorders,* edited by S. Leiblum and R. Rosen, 1–17. New York: Guilford Press, 1988.

Lessa, N. R., and W. F. Scanlon. *Wiley Concise Guides to Mental Health: Substance Use Disorders*. Hoboken, NJ: John Wiley and Sons, 2006.

Mackesy-Amiti, M. E., M. Fendrich, and T. P. Johnson. "Prevalence of Recent Illicit Substance Use and Reporting Bias among MSM and Other Urban Males." *Addictive Behaviors* 33 (2008): 1055–60.

Makadon, H. J., K. H. Mayer, J. Potter, and H. Goldhammer. *The Fenway Guide to Lesbian, Gay, Bisexual, and Transgender Health*. Philadelphia: American College of Physicians, 2008.

Mansergh, G., D. W. Purcell, R. Stall, M. McFarlane S. Semaan, J. Valentine, and R. Valdiserri. "CDC Consultation on Methamphetamine Use and Sexual Risk Behavior for HIV/STD Infection: Summary and Suggestions." *Public Health Reports* 121 (2006): 127–32.

Marlatt, G. A., and D. M. Donovan. *Relapse Prevention*. New York: Guilford Press, 2005.

Martin, P. R., B. A. Weinberg, and B. K. Bealer. *Healing Addiction*. Hoboken, NJ: John Wiley and Sons, 2007.

McLellan, A. T. "What We Need Is a System." In *Rethinking Substance Abuse*, edited by W. R. Miller and K. M. Carroll, 275–92. New York: Guilford Press, 2006.

Mercer, D. E., and G. E. Woody. *An Individual Drug Counseling Approach to Treat Cocaine Addiction*. Bethesda, MD: U.S. Department of Health and Human Services, 1999.

Miller, W. R., and K. M. Carroll. *Rethinking Substance Abuse*. New York: Guilford Press, 2006.

Muller, M. "NIDA-Funded Studies Shed Light on Neurobiology of Drug Craving." *NIDA Notes* 11 (1996): 3–4.

National Institute on Drug Abuse. *Principles of Drug Addiction Treatment: A Research-Based Guide*. Bethesda, Maryland: National Institutes of Health, 2009.

———. *The Science of Addiction*. Bethesda, MD: National Institutes of Health, 2007.

———. *Therapy Manuals for Drug Addiction: A Cognitive-Behavioral Approach: Treating Cocaine Addiction*. Bethesda, MD: U.S. Department of Health and Human Services, 1998.

———. *Therapy Manuals for Drug Addiction: An Individual Counseling Approach to Treat Cocaine Addiction*. Bethesda, MD: U.S. Department of Health and Human Services, 1998.

———. *Topics in Brief: Methamphetamine Addiction: Cause for Concern— Hope for the Future*. Bethesda, MD: National Institutes of Health, 2007.

Nichols, M., and M. Shernoff. "Therapy with Sexual Minorities." In *Principles and Practice of Sex Therapy*, edited by S. Leiblum, 379–415. New York: Guilford Press, 2007.

Nowinski, J., and S. Baker. *The Twelve-Step Facilitation Handbook*. San Francisco: Jossey-Bass Publishers, 1992.

O'Farrell, T. J., and W. Fals-Stewart. *Behavioral Couples Therapy for Alcoholism and Drug Abuse*. New York: Guilford Press, 2006.

Olson, E. D. "Gay Teens and Substance Use Disorders: Assessment and Treatment." *Journal of Gay and Lesbian Psychotherapy* 3 (2000): 69–80.

Orloff, E. "Can Marriage Survive Addiction?" *Counselor*, May 31, 2001, www.counselormagazine.com/feature-articles-mainmenu-63/55-family/199-can-marriage-survive-addiction (accessed July 1, 2010).

Osborne, D. *Suicide Tuesday*. New York: Carroll and Graf Publishers, 2005.

Ostrow, D. G., and R. D. Shelby. "Psychoanalytic and Behavioral Approaches to Drug-Related Sexual Risk Taking: A Preliminary Conceptual and Clinical Integration." *Journal of Gay and Lesbian Psychotherapy* 3 (2000): 129–39.

Peterson, C. "The Future of Optimism." *American Psychologist* 55 (2000): 44–55.

Rosario, W., E. W. Schrimshaw, and J. Hunter. "Predictors of Substance Use Over Time among Gay, Lesbian, and Bisexual Youths: An Examination of Three Hypotheses." *Addictive Behaviors* 29 (2004): 1623–31.

Rotgers, F., J. Morgenstern, and S. T. Walters. *Treating Substance Abuse*. New York: Guilford Press, 2003.

Rubin, E. "Integration of Theory, Research, and Practice: A Clinician's Perspective." In *Treating Substance Abuse,* edited by F. Rotgers, J. Morgenstern, and S. T. Walters, 343–63. New York: Guilford Press, 2003.

Ryan, C. *Supportive Families, Healthy Children: Helping Families with Lesbian, Gay, Bisexual and Transgender Children*. San Francisco: Marian Wright Edelman Institute, San Francisco State University, 2009.

Sandor, R. S. *Thinking Simply about Addiction*. New York: Jeremy P. Tarcher/ Penguin, 2009.

Seligman, M. E. *Authentic Happiness*. New York: Free Press, 2002.

Seligman, M. E., and M. Csikszentmihalyi. "Positive Psychology: An Introduction." *American Psychologist* 55 (2000): 5–14.

Sexuality Information and Education Council of the United States (SIECUS). *Guidelines for Comprehensive Sexuality Education*. New York: SIECUS, 2004.

Stall, R., J. P. Paul, G. Greenwood, L. Pollack, E. Bein, G. M. Crosby, T. C. Mills, D. Binson, T. J. Coates, and J. A. Catania. "Alcohol Use, Drug Use and Alcohol-Related Problems among Men Who Have Sex with Men: The Urban Men's Health Study." *Addiction* 96 (2001): 1589–1601.

Stone A. L., C. L. Storr, and J. C. Anthony. "Evidence for a Hallucinogen Dependence Syndrome Developing Soon after Onset of Hallucinogen Use during Adolescence." *International Journal of Methods in Psychiatric Research* 15 (2006): 116–30.

Urschel, H. C. *Healing the Addicted Brain*. Naperville, IL: Sourcebooks, 2009.

Velasquez, M. M., G. G. Maurer, C. Crouch, and C. C. DiClemente. *Group Treatment for Substance Abuse*. New York: Guilford Press, 2001.

Weiss, R. *Cruise Control*. Los Angeles: Alyson Books, 2005.

White, W. L. "Interviews with Pioneers." *Counselor* 11 (2010): 38–48.

Whitten, L. "Treatment Curbs Methamphetamine Abuse among Gay and Bisexual Men." *NIDA Notes* 20, no. 4 (2006).

Wong, C. F., M. D. Kipke, and G. Weiss. "Risk Factors for Alcohol Use, Frequent Use, and Binge Drinking among Young Men Who Have Sex with Men." *Addictive Behaviors* 33 (2008): 1012–20.

Wong, W., J. Chaw, C. K. Kent, and J. D. Klausner. "Risk Factors for Early Syphilis among Gay and Bisexual Men Seen in an STD Clinic: San Francisco, 2002–2003." *Sexually Transmitted Diseases* 32 (2005): 458–63.

Ziegler, P. P. "Treating Gay, Lesbian, Bisexual, and Transgender Professionals with Addictive Disease." *Journal of Gay and Lesbian Psychotherapy* 3 (2000): 59–68.

# ABOUT THE AUTHOR

MICHAEL SHELTON is director of adult sexual services with Equilibria Psychological and Consultation Services in Philadelphia. He worked at some of the most esteemed treatment facilities in the country, is a frequent contributor to *Psychology Today* on male sex and sexuality issues, and wrote three previous books on human sexuality, including *Boy Crazy*, an examination of gay male monogamy. His passion is bridging the chasm between the fields of addictions treatment and sex & sexuality research.